A Rainbow Book

Carbuying 101

How To Buy a Car with the Change in Your Ashtray

Robert M. Blazak

Library of Congress Cataloging-In-Publication Data

Blazak, Robert M., 1942-
    Carbuying 101 : how to buy a car with the change in your ashtray /
Robert M. Blazak.
    p. cm.
    ISBN 1-56825-066-5
    1. Automobiles--Purchasing. I. Title
TL162.B57   1997
629.222'029'6--dc21

97-17056
CIP

Car-Buying 101:
How To Buy a Car With the Change in Your Ashtray
Copyright 1997 © Carbuyer Consultants, Inc.

Published by:
Rainbow Books, Inc.
P. O. Box 430
Highland City, FL 33846-0430 USA
Editorial Offices Telephone/Fax (941) 648-4420,
Email: NAIP@aol.com
Individual Orders:
Telephone (800) 356-9315, Fax (800) 242-0036

Illustrations used with permission from the artist, Larry Werber.
Cover and interior design by Betsy A. Lampé

Manufactured in the United States of America.

Dedication

To my loving wife, Connie, who has encouraged my crusade.
To Susan, Ruth, Gino and Larry, who have helped with the
writing, editing and content. And to my little grandson, Cody,
who knows all about cars and trucks.

Contents

Preface

I am not writing this book to crucify the auto industry. Like any business, they're in it to make money. What I am trying to do is give the consumer both some knowledge with which to bargain and the facts to deal with auto dealerships which take advantage of uninformed buyers. I have seen too many young people scraping to get off the ground only to be buried in car payments they can't afford. From there, it goes right down hill. The more affluent you are, the more likely you're going to be taken for the proverbial ride.

Dealerships and car lots are not going to like this book. But YOU have a right to know what you are buying and to have the information to negotiate the best buy for you.

How much money the dealership makes IS your business when it comes to YOUR money. If a dealer sold a car at HIS purchase price, he would still make a profit. Remember that as you read through this book.

A dealer can stay in business selling at invoice price. How? Because of kickbacks or holdbacks paid by the manufacturer. He also makes profits from add-ons, financing, trade sales, warranties and service.

The advice given here is aimed at the average car buyer and can be adjusted up or down, depending on the class of vehicle you want to buy. The information is meant to be flexible to give you the bargaining power you desire. Use it, and I promise that you'll be happily surprised at just how much money you can save yourself.

Fifteen years of experience is condensed in this book. While it is a reader-friendly book, easy to understand, I have also added some personal experiences to demonstrate how unique the car industry is.

By the time you finish the last chapter, you should have enough new knowledge to enter your next car-buying experience with confidence, properly prepared for the battle ahead, and come out the winner, both financially and emotionally!

Introduction

Are you INTIMIDATED by car sales associates (both men and women) when it comes to buying a car? Do you feel terrified at the thought of facing this bully who, with his knowledge and professional wit, is going to take you and your checkbook for a royal one-way trip?

The following chapters are designed to help you even the score. You'll learn just what your opponent is about to do and say, and how to defend yourself against every trick in their book. You'll learn how much markup there is on new and used cars, and how to chop it down to a fair profit margin. You will also learn how to CONTROL the finance manager and persuade him to lower interest rates, reduce the cost of warranties and even shorten the length of your contract.

In other words, I'm going to teach you how this mystical adversary thinks, how he or she is taught, and how to keep control of the entire buying adventure.

Once you have learned the tricks of the trade, you'll have the knowledge to reduce the cost of your new purchase by thousands of dollars. Further, you will have the self-confidence and determination — the tools — to put to use what you have learned here.

Additional help is not far away for those who may need support. If, after you read this book, you still feel that you need a crusader at your side, please feel free to contact CARBUYER CONSULTANTS, INC., P. O. Box 770, Roswell, Georgia 30075. My trained staff will answer your questions, give you values on new and used vehicles and consult with you on procedures.

Remember, the purpose of this book and my personal crusade is to give YOU, the consumer, the knowledge necessary to defend yourself, and your money, against the experienced professional, who has been trained in the art of "taking you for a ride."

You can't win a duel with an empty gun. This book is your ammunition.

_____Chapter One

Be Prepared

As an Eagle Scout, I have always lived by the motto:

BE PREPARED.

This is especially true when it comes to buying a car.

Before you start shopping, there are several things you must do:

Decide on exactly what kind of vehicle you want. This includes the following:

1. Sedan, coupe, pickup, station wagon, van, hatchback, convertible, etc.;

2. Import or domestic;

3. Color;

4. 4-cylinder, 6-cylinder, 8-cylinder;

5. Automatic transmission, standard-shift 4-speed or 5-speed;

6. Two-wheel drive, four-wheel drive, all-wheel drive;

7. Style side, flare side, king cab, club cab, pickup trucks.

Chose the options you want. Remember, many are grouped in packages. Consider the following:

1. Air conditioning (not standard on all cars);

2. AM/FM, cassette player, compact disc player;

3. Anti-lock brakes;

4. Cruise control;

5. Floor mats (not standard on all cars);

6. Wheel covers, alloy wheels, locking hubs;

7. Seating — power driver seat only, six-way power, bench, captain's chairs, heated, split-bench, reclining, leather;

8. Tilt steering wheel, leather-wrapped steering wheel;

9. Flip-top roof, sun roof, moon roof, power moon roof;

10. Trailer hitch, towing package;

11. Tinted windows;

12. Leather or cloth interior;

13. Monotone or two-tone paint;

14. Conventional or temporary spare tire;

15. Standard or all-season tires;

16. Rear window defogger;

17. Standard or dual gas tanks;

18. Theft systems;

19. Power door locks, keyless entry;

20. Power windows and mirrors;

21. Remote control trunk lid and fuel door releases;

22. Fog lamps.

You'll need to know what your budget can handle. Don't spin your wheels shopping for a car that's out of your price range. You need to determine what you can afford, and NEVER let anyone push you beyond that limit, NOT EVEN A DOLLAR!

Talk to your bank and credit union, and find out what their interest rates are for new and used cars over 36, 48 and 60 months. This will be vital when you get to the finance office. Start with your own bank and shop by phone. Rates vary for bank and time.

If you're shopping for a used car, you need to tell them how old the car will be that you plan to buy. Interest rates and payment periods vary, based on the age of the car. Older cars might be limited to a 24 month or a 36-month pay off.

Get yourself pre-approved for your loan, if you can. This will give you more clout when you get to the finance office. You can use the pre-approved credit and interest rate to negotiate even better terms.

Locate and take with you the following:

1. Title to your trade, if you're trading a vehicle;

2. Payment book, if you still have payments due on your trade;

3. Insurance card for auto insurance on your trade (be sure it has the name and phone number of your agent);

4. Registration on your trade;

5. Check book and $100 cash for possible deposit;

6. Information, phone numbers, addresses for credit application;

7. Notes on your options;

8. Calculator, pen, paper;

9. Any car books you have read (*Consumer Reports*,

Edmund's, etc.).

Now you're ready to start shopping. If you find what you want, you are ready to do business. Remember: The car you decide to buy tomorrow just might be the car someone else bought yesterday.

By the way, do you know anyone who owns a Fiat? I just found out what the letters F I A T stand for, and from personal experience, I agree:

FIX IT AGAIN, TONY!

Only $199 down, $199 per month gets you into a like-new Mercedes!

199-month, open-end lease, some restrictions may apply, $300 security deposit, first and last months' payments at signing plus $8,000 down payment. 40 cents per mile over 5,000 miles per year. With approved credit. Only two in stock.

Chapter Two

Beware of Advertising

I strongly believe that, when it comes to advertising, the auto industry pushes the limits of deception farther than any other industry. Many of their ads are outright misleading and appear to offer things which just don't exist.

The television ads you see hourly have one thing in common: They generally refer to monthly payments. These payments imply that you can BUY a car with little or nothing down and the small monthly payment indicated in bold, easy-to-read numbers. However, their disclaimers, which are tiny, lengthy, and only on the screen for seconds, state that these prices relate to a lease and require a down payment, security deposit, first and last payment in advance and sometimes other charges.

I have seen ads for new cars for as little as $199 per month on a $20,000 car that imply to the viewer that they can purchase this car for nothing down and $199 per month. In reality, upon reading the disclaimer on stop-action video tape and a large screen, it was a lease with first and last payment, $300 security deposit and $8,000 down payment.

You might as well offer a new Mercedes-Benz SL for $199 a month with a disclaimer requiring a $40,000 security deposit. I'm sure that dozens of people would rush to the dealership to take advantage of this special, only to discover the truth and disappointment.

Many times the ads will show a specific car with a great price that you can actually buy. However, down in the tiny, unreadable disclaimer will be a stock number for that car. And guess what? When you rush down to the dealer, it has just sold. If the car had been there, it would be a basic model with no air, 4 cylinder, standard shift and, probably, orange or yellow. Get the picture?

Another gimmick is to offer you a guaranteed minimum of $2,000 for your trade-in, no matter what the condition. Here you are with a piece of junk in your driveway that may or may not make a return trip to the dealership. But don't get too excited. They'll be glad to pick it up, if you'll buy a new car from them. And, of course, on that new car, they'll load up the price. They've got you hooked!

Beware of ads! Look at the newspaper ads carefully. Most ads usually work the same way. Tiny stock number; tiny disclaimers. This all sets the buyer up for the infamous BAIT AND SWITCH routine, which is:

"We don't have that car in stock, but let me show you something better. Since you're here, and you need a car, we have exactly what you need."

Now that you've been warned, BUYER BEWARE.

With reference to new- and used-car dealerships which offer NO HAGGLE PRICING (i. e. Saturn, CarMax, etc.), my advice is to AVOID THEM LIKE THE PLAGUE!

Any time you can't negotiate the price of a car, you'll pay too much for it. The only way you might get around these locked-in prices is to include a trade in your deal. By negotiating the trade price well above its retail price you can offset some of the overpricing on the car you want to buy.

Buying a car from a personal classified ad in a newspaper can be a real hassle, too. Keep in mind that people generally try to sell a car themselves, because they can't get what they THINK it's worth in the trade. People get attached to their cars like pets. Remember: If someone is selling a car, there's a reason. If the car was in perfect condition, they'd probably keep it. They have no mechanical backup like a dealership would have, no financing, no office to do the paperwork and no reputation to protect.

I once tried to help a friend buy a car from an individual who had advertised in the newspaper. We went and looked at the car, drove it, and even had it checked out by a mechanic. We negotiated the price to about $200 under rough book wholesale. The owner of the for-sale car said, "I've lost the title, but I'll apply for a new one and get it to you shortly."

My friend insisted on buying the car that day, much against my advice. He wrote the seller a $4,500 check, payment in full for the car.

One day later the check was cashed. But after two weeks the seller still had no title. To make a long story short, the man disappeared. When we checked, we discovered the car had three VIN numbers on it. My friend was stuck with a stolen car for which he had paid in full.

Buying or selling cars through the classified ads can be a nightmare. I'll cover the options in a later chapter. I will note here, though, that if you advertise your car in the paper or *Auto Trader*, you must put in a phone number. Be careful of giving up your privacy. You may find yourself dickering with unsavory individuals who don't have the money. Further still, selling your car yourself could cause you to miss out on some sales incentives at the dealership.

One last piece of advice. No matter with whom you're dealing: The only thing that leaves a deposit on a car is a pigeon.

If you ever see an ad for a Rolls Canardly, don't waste your time checking it out. I found out that it's a car that rolls downhill but "can 'ardly" get up the other side. (Thanks, Amy.)

Now I know when the dealerships are desperate to sell. When I go in, I'll be the one in control, and I'll save lots of money, too.

————————————Chapter Three

Timing Is Everything

Choosing the right time to buy a car can save you hundreds of dollars. The time of the year, the days of the month and even the time of the day are all important in purchasing power.

Let's start with the time of the year. At the end of the model year, the dealerships are faced with a dilemma. Each lot has a limit on how many cars they can carry. To receive new cars, they must have room. No room; no cars.

This creates a buyers' market; the dealership must move cars to make room for new cars. Without new cars on their lots, customers will go elsewhere. Therefore, rather than have you go elsewhere, dealerships will discount cars in an effort to move their inventory. Also, the manufacturer will help the dealer by offering FACTORY REBATES. These rebates come directly from the manufacturer to the buyer. Keep this in mind.

Within minutes after you purchase that new car, you will have a car that is a one-year-old used car, and the resale value comes crashing down.

This could be okay, if you drive above average mileage. AVERAGE ANNUAL MILEAGE ON A CAR IS 15,000 miles. This will give you an extra 15,000 miles to drive without having excessive mileage on your car that would depreciate its value substantially. I'll explain this in more detail in a later chapter.

Now for the best days of the month in which to buy a car. Dealers establish a quota each month that is reported to the manufacturer. This tells the manufacturer how many cars they expect to sell that month. The manufacturer uses this information to schedule his production. If the dealer meets the quota, the dealership is rewarded with a kickback or hold-back payment. This could be as much as 5 percent of the total sales for the month. Do the math. That's a lot of money.

If the dealership is approaching the end of the month and is behind on its projection (and they usually are), the dealership will sacrifice cars to meet their quota. Therefore: THE BEST DAYS TO BUY A NEW CAR ARE THE LAST TWO DAYS OF THE MONTH.

Now why, you may well ask, would it matter what time of day you purchase a car? It seems there's some mysterious rule that anyone who buys a car must be held captive for a minimum of three hours to make the sale. This keeps the salesperson in control and makes you pay ANYTHING just to get out of the dealership.

Sales personnel work outrageous hours at their craft, and

12-hour days are not uncommon. By eight or nine o'clock, they're ready to pack it up. THE BEST TIME OF DAY TO DEAL IS JUST BEFORE CLOSING.

Go in about two hours before closing and take your test drive. By the time you're ready to negotiate, it's time to go home. Now you have control; you don't have time to come back. CONTROL is the name of the game. This translates into savings for you.

Now here's the perfect situation. Go in at seven o'clock in the evening on the last day of the month during the introduction of the new models. We're talking hundreds of bucks here. So, do listen up!

This brings up another unique situation — buying a new car when the new cars are first introduced. Let me relate to you a personal experience I had with a client. It points out a potential savings.

When the Mazda Miata was introduced in 1990, a client called me and asked if I could speed up the delivery of her new car. I met her at the dealership and found that she was on a waiting list for incoming Miatas. The dealer was charging full retail (MSRP) plus $2,000 AVAILABILITY CHARGE.

MSRP stands for **Manufacturer's Suggested Retail Price.** Another name for MSRP is **Monroney Sticker.** Knowing the market and how some dealers operate, I checked the inventory on another dealer's computer. I learned that the dealer in question had 42, yes, that's right, 42 new Miatas stored in their back lot. This dealership was intentionally creating a shortage.

If your vanity is so strong that you can't wait 30 days and MUST have the first new car on the road, then you must pay the extra $2,000. Remember: That $2,000 is not reflected on the trade-in value. It's an outright donation to the dealer's vacation fund.

The lady got her new Miata that night for $500 under the MSRP, once I pointed out to the dealer what I had learned.

You can also stop by a dealership and check the location of the salesperson. If you walk in and no salesperson greets you, it's the first week of the month. If someone says, "Hello, can I help you?" it's the second week of the month. If a salesperson greets you in the parking lot, it's the third week of the month. And if three people jump you at the curb, it's time to shop!

My darling Betsy – the best car I ever owned. How can she be worth only $1,500? She's only 10 years old and is clean as a whistle. But she does have 150,000 miles on her . . .

_____Chapter Four

Preparing Your Trade

One problem people seem to have with their trade-in is this: Because their car's been part of their life for so long, they think it's worth a lot more than it really is. When it's time to sell or trade your little gem, it's also time to come down to earth.

With few exceptions, your trade is only worth what a wholesaler will pay for it. When you trade your car at a dealership, about 80 percent of the cars taken as trade-ins are sold off to wholesalers who, in turn, sell them to independent used car lots, take them to auctions or ship them out of the country.

The value of your trade-in is based on a little black book that is compiled and printed weekly by The Hearst Corporation. It's called, THE BLACK BOOK OFFICIAL USED CAR MARKET GUIDE WEEKLY. You can subscribe to it yourself by writing to National Auto Research, P. O. Box 758,

Gainesville, Georgia 30503-0758, and spending $77 (in Georgia add 4 percent sales tax). This book goes back seven years, is updated weekly and is available in your local library.

There's another book, THE BLACK BOOK OFFICIAL OLD CAR MARKET GUIDE, which comes out monthly. This book covers cars from eight to 14 years old and costs $51 per year (add 4 percent sales tax in Georgia). With these books, you can be the hit of the party by telling everyone what *their* car is REALLY worth.

The condition of your trade has very little effect on the Black Book value. To the wholesaler and the used car manager (who usually appraises the trades), this book is their Bible. Here are some DO's and DON'Ts which relate to your trade:

1. DON'T put money in your trade to repair dents and scratches;

2. DON'T polish or wax your trade;

3. DON'T spend money repairing anything that doesn't directly relate to **vital** functions of the car;

4. DON'T buy new tires, wipers, windshields, mirrors, antennas, seat covers, etc.;

5. DO take the beer cans and magazines out of the trunk;

6. DO tie the trunk lid down;

7. DO swap any good tires out with a friend and make a buck or two;

8. DO put a couple cans of STP in the engine if you hear a knock;

9. DO swap out a good stereo radio with a friend;

10. DO sell your trailer hitch if you can get it off; and

11. DO run it through a cheap car wash before taking it in for an appraisal.

These suggestions will help you minimize your losses. You'll never recoup your money if you try to improve the value of your trade-in by making expensive repairs. *The BLACK BOOK rules.*

If the dealership decides to keep the car for resale, they will have it professionally cleaned and detailed, repair what needs to be repaired, and they can do it a lot cheaper than you can do it!

By the way, for those of you who are pickup lovers, BLACK BOOK OFFICIAL USED TRUCK AND VAN GUIDE runs $61 (add 4 percent sales tax, if living in Georgia) and comes out semimonthly.

If you can drive a car onto a lot, it's worth at least $200. It may be the best way to get rid of an old clunker. This can also give you a down payment which, though small, can be helpful when it comes to your financing.

My uncle's car was so old that the license plate was written in Roman numerals. But it still had some trade-in value.

She was made just for you . . .

_____Chapter Five

Don't Get Attached

One of the common mistakes car buyers make when they start shopping is to find a car and fall in love with it. This puts the salesperson in the driver's seat and allows him or her to control the sale. Keep in mind that there are other cars at other dealerships that are just as nice as the one you've found.

Salespeople have several techniques they use to help you fall in love with a car. One is called, "Puppydogging." This urges you to take the car home for the evening, while they shop your trade for a better price. The idea is that after you drive it for a while and show it to your friends, it will be more difficult to give it back. Beware of this technique and don't get emotionally involved. It could cost you time, money and heartbreak.

Another gimmick is: THE TEST DRIVE. Most salespeople have a planned route and presentation in their program. They use subliminal sales as you maneuver YOUR new car over THEIR obstacle course. Turn YOUR car left at the light. Try YOUR radio. YOUR headlights. YOUR windows. YOUR power seats. Pull over here, and let's check out YOUR trunk. By the time you get back to the dealership, you're driving YOUR car.

The easiest way to break this pattern is to ask to take the car on the freeway to see how it handles at freeway speeds. You can also listen for road noise and engine sounds, and you can feel the engine pick up and check the braking ability. Also, check the vision in all directions. Ask questions. Keep control.

It is the salesperson's job to sell you a car from inventory. If he or she doesn't have exactly what you want, he or she must convince you to buy what is available. A car is probably the second most expensive thing you will buy, next to a home. You'll be driving it for at least a couple of years. Get exactly what YOU want.

Regarding new cars, every dealer has a computer that is connected to every other dealership in their region. In seconds, the inventory of each of these dealers can be pulled up on a computer screen. This information is updated daily.

If the car you want is out there, the dealer can locate it. They can do what's called a "Dealer Transfer" and exchange cars to bring in YOUR choice. This can usually be done within 24 hours and does not cost you anything but a little time. Let the dealership EARN your business.

With used cars, your choices may be more limited. Stick to your plan and don't settle for something that doesn't meet your needs.

While selling used cars many years ago, my manager offered a bonus to any salesperson who could sell an old yellow Mustang that had been on the lot for months. A young couple came in looking for a good buy. I showed them this mustard-yellow antique. I convinced them that it was a limited issue, and it would probably go up in value soon. They believed me and jumped on the opportunity.

Maybe that's why I'm in the consulting business today. To make up for having been a car salesman.

Why, we'll just give that darned old car fella a thing or two to think about. For all he knows, I'm Matt Dillon comin' to even up the score. That sidewindin', snake-eyed . . .

Chapter Six

Don't Go Alone

This chapter addresses an all too common problem: SEXUAL DISCRIMINATION.

In the auto industry, I believe this is a serious problem. When a woman goes into a dealership alone, you can hear the hive start to hum.

Car salesmen have a reputation for assuming that ALL women are absent of any knowledge of cars. They are, in essence, easy pickings for high profits and commissions.

Both women and men must be tough negotiators and prepared to handle these misguided salespeople. These salespeople are about as useful as a turn signal on a dragster.

The first thing to do is to prepare yourself, using the information provided in Chapter One. The fact that you're reading this book is an indication that you are aware of how important it is to stay one step ahead of the salesperson. Collect all the data you can on the car of your dreams. Read this book twice and underline, if you need to.

Remember the Number One rule: Any time you lose control or feel uncomfortable, BACK OFF or LEAVE and start over another day. Any time you get pressured, remind the salesperson that he/she has competitors all over town.

I know this sounds unusual, but take someone along with you. He or she doesn't have to know a Bronco from a Cobra. The salesperson won't know that. It will just keep that salesperson on tiptoes and give you more control. Besides, two against one are better odds in your favor.

When I was selling cars, I was appalled by the attitudes of most of the so-called professional salespeople with whom I worked. Men and women alike. It didn't matter where I worked — Ford, Pontiac, Chrysler, imports. Even today, as I visit dealerships around the south, I still experience the same attitudes. Don't be afraid of putting these people in their place.

The judge was very stern with the woman. "You are the wife of this man," he said severely. "You knew he was a car salesman when you married him?"

"Yes," she replied. "I was getting old and had to choose between a car salesman, a burglar and a lawyer. He was the only one on parole at the time!"

Dealers, dealers everywhere,
and nary a car that's cheap.
There are name-brand lots
and lots that confuse,
just stay away from the
small-time lot ruse.

------------- Chapter Seven

Where To Buy

For those of you who are buying NEW CARS, the rules are simple. Shop in dealerships which are convenient to you. Once you are prepared, as in Chapter One, you can go, at your convenience, and cruise the **new car dealerships** which are selling the cars in which you're most interested.

Don't be concerned about the service department at this point. The service department is a separate profit center. Any dealer that sells the same brand of car that you're buying will give you good service, no matter where you bought the car. Service on your car is not limited to one dealership, and warranty service is honored at any dealership in the country. Selling their service department to get you to buy at their dealership is just another ploy to keep you from shopping elsewhere.

Shopping for USED CARS requires a little more thought. If you are looking for a car priced over $5,000, shop ONLY at new car dealerships which have a used car inventory. There are good reasons for this. They are:

1. They only keep quality trade-ins from new car buyers. Generally, about 60 percent of their used cars are selected trades.

2. The remainder often come from other dealers who take trade-ins of brands that match that dealership's brand.

3. Wholesalers buy the unwanted cars and sell them off to small used car lots or ship them out of state or out of the country.

4. The new car dealership has the equipment and trained staff to properly recondition a trade cosmetically and mechanically.

5. They can often include limited warranties on their cars at no extra cost.

6. Because the dealership represents a major brand of car, they are more protective of their reputation than the small, independent used car lot.

7. The dealership has the same financial sources available to the used car buyer as it does to the new car buyer. This benefit can often save you hundreds of dollars in interest.

8. They will often take your trade to other dealers and wholesalers to try to get you more trade-in value.

9. They generally have a better atmosphere for doing business,

more professional personnel and cleaner bathrooms. (Remember the mystical three-hour purchase minimum we discussed earlier in the book!)

Another source for used cars is from INDIVIDUALS. Sometimes you can find a lucky buy. But consider these problems:

1. Many people who are selling their own vehicles are trying to get full retail price because they think it's worth much more than they can get as a trade-in.

2. They are often trying to get full retail price because they owe more on the car than it's worth.

3. Scheduling time to see the car can be very time consuming. Time is money.

4. Locating the car can be a nightmare.

5. You must pay cash or set up your own financing.

6. If you have a trade, you still must sell it yourself. You lose the benefits of the trade-in regarding loan payoff and refinancing.

7. You still must arrange to have it inspected, which can mean another appointment and more travel time.

8. You must handle the registration of the vehicle yourself.

9. You must deal with title and license transfers yourself. In some states that can become involved.

Another question that is common, "Can I get a better deal in the city or in the country?" Dealerships in the city carry a much higher overhead than the old country stores. But they can offset that with higher volume. Country dealerships have low overhead, but their sales volume is lower. So — it's a draw.

Shop where it is convenient. With the knowledge you are acquiring here, you can get a good deal anywhere.

As you can see, WHERE you buy is an important consideration. My best advice is to AVOID THE JALOPY JUNGLES and individuals. Shop the CONVENIENT DEALERSHIP nearest to you.

Here's a tip for you Yugo owners who want to get top dollar when you trade in your car. To **double** the value of your trade — FILL THE GAS TANK!

The well-prepared customer arms himself with information.

‑‑‑‑‑‑‑‑‑‑‑‑‑‑‑‑Chapter Eight

Finding Information

There are other sources for information on new and used cars that can be acquired. I've discussed the books available from NATIONAL AUTO RESEARCH in a previous chapter. These books will give you current prices on USED cars and trucks. If you can't afford to subscribe to them, just go to your local library and look up the information you require there.

For you NEW car buyers, there's another book offered by NATIONAL AUTO RESEARCH called BLACK BOOK OFFICIAL NEW CAR INVOICE GUIDE. It is revised monthly and costs $69.00 annually (add 4 percent Georgia sales tax). The address is P. O. Box 758, Gainesville, Georgia 30503-0758 or phone toll free 800-554-1026 (in Georgia 800-848-6460). This book is also available in your local library.

For information on new cars, there are several good sources. One of the best is CONSUMER REPORTS ANNUAL

AUTO ISSUE offered every April. Another source of valuable new car information is THE CAR BOOK by Jack Gillis, published annually by Harper & Row, Publishers, Inc. These books cover safety features, maintenance comparisons, fuel economy, warranties and many other aspects of most new car on the market.

Another NEW CAR price book available in bookstores and libraries is EDMUND'S NEW CAR PRICES, published by Edmund Publications Corp. This book compares to the BLACK BOOK on pricing and includes pictures of the cars.

There are many other good sources of information besides those mentioned. You can go to your local dealer and pick up brochures on your car choices. Compare this year's model with last year's. You might discover there are no changes and last year's car might be a better deal.

There is a good reason why I suggest you find your own sources for wholesale prices on new cars. I have worked for dealers who have made their own invoices on new cars and mixed them with the factory invoices. I have personally seen as many as five invoices per car with varying prices, ranging from $200 to $2,000 over the *real* factory invoice.

Some are increased by adding fictitious items and prices. Some just change the arithmetic, so that it can be blamed on a computer — if caught by the buyer. Some are just whited out and changed. Many of these bogus invoices are printed on blank manufacturer's invoices.

I realize that there are only a small percentage of dealers who fraudulently make up these invoices. But they do exist, and you should be aware of them. If you can't get access to the price books mentioned in this chapter, price shop with other dealers. Just like going to a doctor — get another opinion.

When you go in to buy your car, take all of this information with you. A knowledgeable, prepared customer is a horrifying sight to a car salesperson. Immediately, the prepared customer has taken away some of the salesperson's control.

Remember, the car salesperson is the real EXPERT. Definition of expert: X is an unknown quantity — and SPURT is a big drip!

Which is the better deal, The $500 cash back or the 4 percent interest rate?

_____Chapter Nine

Rebate, Rebate

There are basically three types of rebates available in the new car market:

1. THE FACTORY REBATE;

2. THE DEALER REBATE; and

3. THE FACTORY-TO-DEALER REBATE.

The **FACTORY REBATE** is the most common. This is a cash rebate directly from the manufacturer to the customer. They generally appear late in the model year as an incentive to help move older new cars off the lots to make room for the incoming new models. This is a DIRECT GIFT TO YOU and should not be included in the negotiating of the new car price.

Many dealers will include this rebate in with the discounted price to make it appear you're getting a better deal than you really are. KEEP IT OUT OF THE DEAL until you have your price agreed upon. Then, subtract it from your negotiated price.

Where do you find out if there is a rebate available and if the rebate advertised is correct? ASK!

Don't ask your salesperson when you start dealing. Call the competition. Call the manufacturer's representative from the yellow pages. Go to the library and get a copy of AUTOMOTIVE NEWS published by Crain Communications, Inc. This is a weekly newspaper published primarily for the dealership industry. It updates rebates, market trends, sales volume production conditions and other information that dealers need to remain competitive.

Do not miss out on this gift. It ranges from $200 to $3,000, depending on the time of the year and the amount of overproduction.

THE DEALER REBATE is a discount from the dealer to the customer. This is usually used for advertising purposes to draw in customers. It is nothing more than a discount off the MSRP (MANUFACTURER'S SUGGESTED RETAIL PRICE). Remember the term: MSRP. It will be popping up throughout the remainder of this book.

Don't confuse these two types of rebates. As you can see, they're not the same.

THE FACTORY-TO-DEALER REBATE is one that the public usually never knows about. From time to time, the manufacturer will put this rebate on slow-moving models which are causing problems with production schedules. This is an incentive for the dealership to push harder to move these overstocked cars. The dealer can pass the rebate on if he needs to.

OPTION PACKAGE DISCOUNTS are not rebates. You'll see these discounts in most advertisements, shown as a special discount off the price of the car. This is HOGWASH!

If you read the window sticker (**MSRP**), you'll see that the option package is already discounted. This discount is the difference between the total cost of buying several items individually and buying them in a group. Most cars are manufactured with groups of options to reduce production cost. This is just another example of deceptive advertising.

$500 REBATE OR 4 PERCENT INTEREST RATE FOR 36 MONTHS! This is a sales tool used by manufacturers to encourage sales when things are slow. The operative words to this gimmick are OR and 36 MONTHS.

First, you need to understand that the dealer is offering either a rebate OR a low interest rate. This option is usually touted by a fast-talking pitch man in television and radio ads and is almost never highlighted in newspaper ads.

Now, you must decide which option is best for you. Will the $500 be more of a savings than the lowered interest rate? Let's use $10,000 as a financed amount and compare. You have already talked to your bank (as in Chapter 1), and your available interest rate is 9 percent.

This offer is limited to a 36-month loan, so payments may be out of your range. $10,000, less the rebate, or $9,500 at 9 percent for 36 months equals $302.10 per month or $10,875.60. Subtract the original principal of $10,000 and that equals $875.60 in interest.

$10,000 at 4 percent for 36 months equals $295.24 per month or $10,628.64 less the principal of $10,000, and that equals $628.64 in interest.

The savings created by the lower interest rate is $875.60 less $628.64 or $246.96. You must ask yourself if the payment of $295.24 will fit your budget or if $9,500 at 9 percent for 60 months ($197.21 per month) is necessary. I always encourage my clients to keep their payment period as short as they can handle. This puts the vehicle in a positive equity position much sooner.

Take your time with this decision and make sure you do what's best for your financial situation. Once you sign the contract, it's very difficult to get out of it.

I suggest that you purchase a PAYMENT BOOK as part of your library. It shows payments based on interest rates from 3 percent to 30 percent and payment periods from 1 year to 50 years. This book is also called an AMORTIZATION SCHEDULE or AMORTIZATION BOOK and is available at most bookstores. It is also useful for calculating mortgages and personal loans. A book that is common and that I use is FINANCIAL MONTHLY MORTGAGE TABLES published by Financial Publishing Company (Publication #589).

Do your homework before you sign papers in the finance office. If you're being rushed, BACK OFF and live to spend another day — wisely.

A recently divorced ex-wife of a well-known talk radio host decided to buy a new car. She picked out and bought the top-of-the-line luxury model. As she was about to drive it away, she noticed that the radio had no buttons on it. Upon returning to the dealer, she asked the salesman how the radio was supposed to work without buttons or dials.

"This is the latest in technology," he explained. "Because so many accidents are caused by people fooling with their radios and not watching the road, we have developed this radio that works on voice command. Just tell it what kind of music you want, and it will respond."

As the woman drove off again, she decided to try out her new car radio. She clearly said, "Country," and, lo and behold, Garth Brooks sang out his latest hit. Then she tried, "Blues!" B. B. King began his latest tune. She was ecstatic.

Suddenly, as she was about to pass through a green light, another car bolted into the intersection and nearly hit her broadside. In her anger, she rolled down the window and shouted at the drive, "Where did you get your driver's license? Sear's catalog? You stupid idiot!"

The blues music stopped. And on her new car radio was her ex-husband's talk radio program.

Think I'll spend my lunch hour listening to one of Bob Blazak's great car-salesman war stories.

_____Chapter Ten

Break Time

This is a good time to break away from the doldrums of facts and education and tell you a war story. In particular, I'd like to tell you about an experience I had when I was just getting started in auto sales.

It was mid-August, and I had been selling Fords for about a month. I had a desk by the front window, which neutralized the air-conditioning but gave me a first look at incoming customers. About 3:00 p.m. the showroom was empty, and the other salesmen were either talking on the phone to their friends or talking to themselves, so to speak, when a vehicle pulled into the lot and parked outside my window.

It was a classic old Chevy pickup truck, complete with dents, rust, spilled paint and ladder rack. A man climbed out of the driver's seat. He was about 6 feet, 6 inches, unshaven, 280 pounds, wore an old t-shirt and bib overalls. He had paint stains from head to toe and the biggest chew of tobacco in his mouth that I'd ever seen. As he exited his truck, he tucked an old wadded grocery bag under his arm. By the time he reached the door, the other salesmen had vanished altogether, except for me.

He wandered to the center of the showroom and stood there chewing and drooling his tobacco. I walked up to him and offered my assistance.

His response, after pausing almost 10 seconds, "Wanna T-Bird, a new 'un."

I invited him to sit down at my desk, while I retrieved an inventory list. He did so, and I quickly returned, list in hand. As I sat down, he pointed out the window at a row of new Thunderbirds across the parking lot. He said, "Want that white 'un."

Since there was only one white Thunderbird in stock, I had the information I needed.

Then, he muttered, "How much?"

I looked down at my inventory sheet and read off the MSRP (Retail Price), added a $169 pre fee, $50 tag and title fee, and sales tax. After totaling it, I looked him square in the eye and said, "$18,457.12 — out the door."

He paused another 10 seconds and said, "Take it." Paused again and added, "Take it outa here." Then, he handed me the brown paper bag from under his arm.

Taken aback, I opened the bag and stared in at more

greenbacks than I'd seen in years. Bundles of mixed bills were wrapped in rubber bands and paperclips. I started sorting and counting as fast as I could. I was fearful he might change his mind. The largest bill was $100; you can see what I was up against with regard to the time factor.

When I had counted out what I thought was $18,457 in bills, I reached into my pocket and threw in 12 cents to top off the total. I would have guess there was still around $5,000 in the brown paper bag. However, not missing a beat, I quickly filled out the necessary paperwork and had him sign where necessary. With that, I rushed the papers and cash to the finance manager and returned with his receipt and other completed forms. Then, I handed him the keys.

The man said, "Pick her up later," nodded his approval, walked out the door, and drove off into the afternoon heat.

What fascinated me most about this whole experience? It has been a 45-minute sale, and he never once spit tobacco!

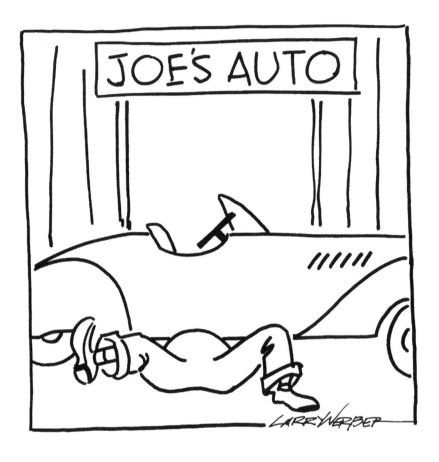

Let's see, here. There's the engine, the radiator, the transmission . . . Oops, no gas tank! Another lemon!

Chapter Eleven

Check It Out

Before you buy a used car, it's imperative that you have it checked out thoroughly by a mechanic OF YOUR CHOICE. Whether you buy from an independent used car lot, from a used car lot connected to a new car dealership, or from an individual, this is very important.

Used cars are generally traded or sold for a reason. It could be mechanical, visual or due to mileage. Not all dealers take the time or money to inspect AND repair a used car properly. The less they can put into a car, the more profit potential. When they do fix the obvious, they usually choose the most cost-effective way possible.

If you find a car that meets your needs and seems like a good buy for you, after keen negotiating, write up a buyer's order and put on it in large print: PENDING MECHANICAL APPROVAL.

This will give you a legal out if your mechanic finds any problems. If the salesman refuses to agree to this documentation, WALK AWAY. HE'S PROBABLY AWARE OF A PROBLEM AND IS HIDING IT.

Unlike new cars, you can't run to the competition and find the same car. You may have to alter your requirements a little, but it's still better than buying a problem car. When you do find the right used car that fits your needs, you must be ready to move quickly. (Review Chapter One.)

I'll give you an example of what can happen by checking out a car on your own.

I met a client at a dealership to negotiate the purchase of a used Jeep Wrangler that he had chosen. It was evening, and we test drove the car. Visual inspection inside the service bay was very positive. It seemed like a good deal.

While inspecting the interior, I rummaged through the glove compartment and found some gas receipts with the former owner's name and address. Since the address was local, I gave him a call from the dealership. He had traded the Wangler in on a new Jeep, and his deal was done. He had no reason not to tell me all the good AND bad about his old car. He also told me what he was given as a trade-in value. But, to my dismay, he advised me that prior to his trading the car, he was four-wheeling in the mountains and bottomed out on some rocks, damaging the undercarriage. It never ran right after that, he said, and it would not align properly.

I explained my findings to my client. Despite the great price, my client walked away from the deal.

If you can't find information on the previous owner on your own, ASK! If the car is a trade-in, and the salesman won't give you a name or phone number, BEWARE!

Some cars arrive at the used car lot from the auctions or wholesalers. They have little or no history, and information is difficult to trace. They still might be good cars, but the odds are lowered. By spending $50 to $75 to have your mechanic inspect your potential purchase, you can overcome this lack of information and minimize your chances of buying a lemon.

Make an appointment with a mechanic in whom you have confidence. If you don't know a reliable mechanic, ask a friend or neighbor for some suggestions. Take your potential new-used car to the mechanic. If the salesperson hesitates about allowing you to do this, something is wrong.

As far as your taking the car off the lot alone, dealerships have insurance to protect them from liability in these situations. You must give them a copy of your driver's license and insurance coverage to protect them. But you can drive alone. THAT GOES FOR TEST DRIVES ALSO.

If you don't remember anything else from this chapter, remember this: It doesn't matter if you're buying a used car from your mother — have it checked out by a good mechanic. Even if it seems to be running fine, something costly could be ready to fail.

Surely you can cut back on groceries to have the car of your dreams. All you've got to come up with is $499 per month!

_____Chapter Twelve

Price — Not Payment

One of the most common ways of confusing the customer and maintaining control is THE TRADE ALLOWANCE.

This technique involves quoting you a price less your trade. It can be used on new and used cars, when a trade is involved. The salesperson will say, "I'll sell you my car for $8,000 and your car."

This is nothing more than a smoke screen to disguise the selling price of the new car and the trade-in value of your trade. When new cars are involved, a rebate may also be hidden.

The best way to overcome this fact is to stop the negotiating and start over on your terms. Separate each part of the transaction and negotiate them one at a time. Then, put them together to formulate your final offer.

As I mentioned in the chapter on rebates, take them aside, until you finalize the value of your trade and the price of the purchase. The rebate is an independent part of the overall picture.

Next, you must negotiate the value of your trade. Again, this is independent of the new car price. What your trade is worth should have nothing to do with the value of the car you are buying.

Finally, the car you are buying should be negotiated, as if there were no trade involved. Each of these procedures is covered in other chapters in this book.

Your goals are to get the lowest price possible on your purchase, the highest price possible on your trade, and all the rebates you are entitled to get. Then, take the new car price and subtract the value of the trade and rebates. Then, add the sales tax based on the difference between the purchase price and the trade-in value. I REPEAT: Sales tax is based on THE DIFFERENCE BETWEEN THE PURCHASE PRICE AND THE TRADE-IN VALUE — not just the purchase price.

If you are buying a car for $15,000, and your trade is worth $8,000, then your sales tax is on $7,000, not $15,000. Sales tax is also based on the county where the car will be based.

We get back to that familiar term — CONTROL. If you don't control the negotiating of all parts of your purchase, it could cost you literally thousands of your hard-earned dollars. Stick to these fundamentals, and you'll do just fine.

I have a rule of thumb that I stand by. It carries throughout this book and all my auto consulting business. I call it: MY 80% RULE.

80% of all dealers are out to get every penny they can from you at any cost;

80% of the salespeople in auto sales are nomadic, inexperienced, money-hungry children;

80% of the cars manufactured (domestic and import) will have problems before the warranty is up; and

80% of the public has little or no knowledge of modern car-buying methods.

This may seem a little harsh, but any time two people can buy the same $14,000 new car and have a different bottom line of $6,000, then the problem is in need of serious review, and the cause is related to 80% of the dealerships, the salespeople and the consumer.

I mention this because I did a television special a couple of years ago about just this problem. And the station chose — AT RANDOM — a dealership and a car. The car had an MSRP of $14,000. Two young ladies, employees of the station, were sent to the dealership to buy the same car. They had identical credit, down payments and ages. They went on different days and were wired for sound. The only variable was that one girl had no experience, and the other girl was trained by me for three hours.

After discounts, rebates and financing, the difference between their deals was almost $6,000. Was this solely the fault of the dealership? I believe the problem involved everyone.

The dealerships seem to believe in "Let the buyer beware." The customer seems to feel it's the fault of the dealerships. The salespeople are just trying to make a living, and the government wants nothing to do with the whole mess.

I strongly believe the answer is in education. If the public would take the time, as you are now doing, to educate themselves on car-buying, the other entities would have to conform. The purchase of a vehicle is often the second most expensive purchase an individual makes in his or her lifetime. It should be taken seriously.

> You're on the right track. The more you learn; the more you save!

And if you buy the car from me today, I'll throw in the gold package and leather seating for no extra charge.

_____Chapter Thirteen

Write It Down

One of the many problems that car buyers call me about is: Not getting things promised them by the salespeople.

Once you take delivery, the attitude toward you changes and promises are forgotten. Whether it's floor mats or body repair, all those cheerful, verbal guarantees are lost in some cosmic void.

Whether you're buying a new or used car, it is very important to put every promise IN WRITING. The place to do this is ON THE BUYER'S ORDER.

Remember, earlier in this book, I said that you should always protect yourself by putting "Pending Mechanical Approval" on the buyer's order. You should also insist that the salesperson write down anything promised. This could include:

1. Body repair;

2. Floor mats;

3. Rear bumpers on pickups;

4. Upgrading radio;

5. Adding air conditioning;

6. Adding CD player;

7. Repairing broken locks;

8. Repairing power doors or windows;

9. Cleaning and servicing the car;

10. Repainting a car;

11. Replacing mirrors;

12. Repairing lights or wipers;

13. Adding pin stripes;

14. Detailing the car;

15. Minor or major mechanical repairs; and

16. Gold packages.

As you can see, there could be several things that need to

be done to make the car a good buy for you. If you negotiate these adjustments into your deal, they MUST be put in writing, or you may have no recourse after the sale. There are some Jekyll and Hydes out there, and you must protect yourself.

I had a lady call me recently who said that she bought a used car from a "reputable" dealership in Atlanta, and the tires were visually in poor condition. The salesperson promised her that they would put new tires on the car at her convenience. After delivery, she went in to have the tires changed out and to her surprise, no one recalled ever making such a promise. The sales manager said, "With the great price you got on that car, we would lose money if we replaced your tires. In good faith, however, we will sell you four tires at OUR COST."

To make things worse, the lady agreed to buy the tires and received retreads at the cost of new tires.

Had she just written on the buyer's order, **Tires to be replaced with new, major-brand tires at dealer's expense**, she would have legal recourse and probably could have avoided the problem all together.

Many dealerships don't want these promises in writing. They will imply that they should be trusted. Look at it as a business. Good business people put everything in writing. You should, too.

For those of you who own AUDIs, why would you want to own a car named for a bellybutton?

I'm keeping the keys to my trade until after we've discussed the price.
No keys; no trade.

_____Chapter Fourteen

Control the Keys

There are many unwritten rules in the auto business. By knowing how auto dealers think and operate, you will have a better chance of regaining CONTROL OF YOUR buying experience.

One of these rules is to innocently put the customer in a position that they can't leave until you, the salesperson AND the sales manager have exhausted every effort to sell you a car. Acquiring and holding the keys to your trade is the easiest way to accomplish this.

As soon as you express an interest in a car, it will be necessary to appraise your trade. The value of your trade is essential to negotiate the purchase of the new or used car you want to buy. You must turn over the keys to your car to the salesperson, so that he or she can have your trade appraised by someone else in the used car department. At this point, your trade and keys are out of your control, and you are dealership-bound.

Standard procedure dictates that when the trade is appraised, the appraisal slip AND your keys are taken to the sales MANAGER and held until the salesperson meets with his manager to discuss pricing. This puts you in the salesperson's office with no opportunity to leave at will. If you decide to drop the negotiations and leave, the salesperson must go to the manager to get your keys, giving him a chance to bring in reinforcements.

The solution is very simple and only requires a little self-confidence. When you sit down in the salesperson's office, explain to him or her that you will be happy to fill out a credit application, while you're waiting, but you would like to have the keys to your trade before you discuss price. He has no reason not to comply with your wishes. No keys; no buy. You must be in a position to leave at YOUR will.

When you receive your keys back, be sure to ask for the exact location of your trade. Having to track it down only gives them time to lean on you harder. Your trade is generally kept in the used car department or parked in some inconvenient location. It is rarely where you left it.

Another unwritten rule used by most dealerships is called, T. O. or TURN OVER RULE. This rule states that NO CUSTOMER CAN LEAVE THE LOT UNTIL THEY HAVE BEEN INTRODUCED (turned over) TO THE "MANAGER."

The sales force is very familiar with this rule. I have seen decent salespeople FIRED for not following this rule. The purpose is to give the manager a chance to either thank you for your purchase or take over the sale and convince you to stay and buy. He wants to see if you're still breathing so he can pull a victory out of the jaws of his salesperson's defeat.

You can expect to be T. O.ed. Just be prepared for it to happen. If you are T. O.ed (ticked off) by the salesperson, you don't need to be T.O.ed again.

Escape to fight another day.

He's no Bronco, but he is one very low-mileage Mule.

Chapter Fifteen

Mileage Mysteries

The question often comes up, "How does mileage affect the value of a car, and what is considered normal?"

Mileage is very important to new and used cars. THE AVERAGE ANNUAL MILEAGE ON A CAR TODAY IS 15,000 MILES PER YEAR. If a three-year-old used car has over 45,000 miles on it, then it is considered to have excessive mileage, and retail and wholesale value is decreased. The higher the mileage, the less the car is worth. How those miles got on the car is NOT a factor.

There is also a major drop in the value of a car when it reaches certain milestones. The rule of thumb is that when domestic cars each 100,000 miles, the value drops significantly. For imports, the magic number is about 150,000 miles. When cars reach these milestones, it is thought that they have peaked in life expectancy and repair costs outweigh the value of the car.

New cars, known as Executive Cars, Top Hats, Demos (Demonstrators) or Loaners are unique. They are NEW cars, not titled, which have from 3,000 to 18,000 miles on them. It's important to separate them from year-old used cars. Since these are not titled cars, they are still actually considered NEW and carry a higher price tag, since they were bought by the dealership at invoice as a NEW unit. These cars are not as good a deal as a year-old used car.

Year-old used cars are cars which were previously owned and taken in on trade at or near used wholesale value. The difference between these cars can be thousands of dollars in purchase price.

Consider this. You buy a NEW car from your friendly dealer and take delivery. You decide you don't want it and drive it directly across the street to another dealer and trade it in on his new car.

The trade-in value of your used car will be $2,000 to $5,000 less than you paid for it as a NEW car. Someone else comes around to buy a car. Which is the better buy? The new car COULD be bought at invoice with full manufacturer's warranty. The used car COULD be bought at USED WHOLESALE VALUE plus a small markup and also have full manufacturer's warranty.

The best buy you can make is to find a ONE-YEAR-OLD USED CAR WITH AVERAGE MILES. I agree that there is a limited supply, but they are out there.

There is still concern about mileage rollbacks on cars. Most states carry a $10,000 fine and possible prison time for those convicted of tampering with odometers. Despite these strict laws, there is still considerable activity in this area.

Having your prospective used car checked out by your mechanic is one way to protect yourself. Also, in your viewing of the car at the dealership, look at the gas and brake peddles for wear. If a car has in excess of 50,000 miles on it, the right side of the brake peddle and the gas peddle will show wear. Also, the carpet at the base of the gas peddle will be worn.

There are still a considerable amount of odometer high-jinks going on. A recent article I read indicated that a high percentage of former rental cars had mileage reductions of 20,000 to 40,000 miles. It's still a BUYER BEWARE world out there. So, be aware.

Mileage charts are available in the price books mentioned earlier. Those books are available in your local library. Consider these charts when pricing your car. The lending institutions and car dealers will value your trade based on these mileage charts.

One further note. High mileage comes from a traveling salesman, as a rule. Because of his trade, and the fact that his car is his office and source of income, traveling salesmen tend to take much better care of their cars than the average owner. They tend to service cars better and keep cars in top shape. If you find a car that has an extra 15,000 or 20,000 miles on it, over the average, it could still be a good buy. Keep in mind, though: When you trade it later, the trade-in value will reflect that high mileage.

This woman was finished with her Christmas shopping, and when she went out to the parking lot, there were four men sitting in the car. She asked them to get out, and they said no, so she repeated, and they still refused. She then put down her packages and pulled the handgun she had for protection, out of her purse. The men got out of her car and fled. She then realized that it wasn't her car; hers was parked 3 spaces away!

The dealer insists that I put down a deposit. I'm taking no more than $100 cash and *I'm* insisting on a receipt.

_____Chapter Sixteen

Cash Deposits

Should I give the dealership a deposit once I have negotiated my deal, and if so, how much?

First, we have to determine just what the deposit is for. Is it to take your choice off the market? Is it to allow the dealer to bring in a dealer trade? Is it to show you are serious about buying a car?

If you are told that you must put down a deposit to hold the car until credit is approved, then, in today's market, I believe that's unnecessary. By signing the buyer's order, you are showing good faith. Since there is no contract, the deposit holds no guarantee that they will hold the car. If they insist that you give them a deposit, it should be no more than $100 and IN CASH. Be sure to get a receipt.

The reason I recommend cash is this. If you give them a

personal check, they can and usually will deposit it immediately, requiring a 10-day waiting period for the check to clear. Then, they will, at their convenience, write you a refund check. This could tie up your deposit for two to three weeks, making it difficult for you to shop elsewhere. By giving them cash, the dealership can refund your money immediately.

If you have properly tagged your buyer's order, PENDING FINANCIAL APPROVAL, you can excuse yourself from the deal, and you are entitled to a refund.

If the dealer has agreed to purchase a car from another dealership, the dealer must actually buy that car and is obligated to keep it in inventory. Even though the dealer is trading out one of his, the car he brings in for you might not be desirable for his inventory or demographics. A smart dealer will not execute the trade until the financing is approved and the customer is satisfied with all aspects of the deal. A deposit in this case is fair. But it should still be limited to $100.

If the salesperson says he wants a deposit to take to his manager to show good faith and to get your proposal approved, JUST SAY, "NO!" It is not necessary or advisable to give anyone a deposit for something that hasn't been decided. Ask the salesperson to give you a deposit to show you that the dealership is dealing with good faith. Who's the customer, anyway?

Before you go around dropping deposits at every dealer in town, do your homework, know what you want, find it, negotiate it to your satisfaction, THEN put down as small a cash deposit, IF ANY, as you can.

In today's market, if you're working with a well-established dealership, about 80% of deposits on canceled deals are refunded sooner or later. Protect yourself by dealing with WELL-ESTABLISHED NEW CAR DEALERSHIPS.

Bumper Sticker:
"Get off the phone and drive!"

**Put that down and come quick!
Bob Blazak is telling another
one of his war stories.**

_ _ _ _ _ _ _ _ _ _ Chapter Seventeen

Break II

You've been working hard and have a lot of information to absorb. Time for a little break. Here's another war story, a memorable experience that occurred when I was selling Pontiacs.

It was a cold wintery morning in February, and the weatherman was predicting even worse weather. The dealership was empty and half the usual sales staff didn't show up. I was sitting in my little cubical, wondering if anyone would bother to shop for cars on such a miserable day.

A man pulled up, parked and came into the showroom carrying a briefcase. He wore a three-piece suit and heavy topcoat. Everyone, including me, ASSUMED he was an ad salesman or selling something to the dealership. He walked up to the receptionist and had to ask for a salesperson. Fortunately, my office was closest, and I responded first.

He introduced himself and sat down across the desk from me. Wasting no time, he took out a piece of paper from his briefcase, placed it in front of me, and said, "This is a list of four stock numbers on cars I found on your lot last night, after you'd closed. Write them up with a $500 discount on each and give me your total out-the-door price. They're for my wife and three children. I live in a 5% tax county."

It took me about 10 minutes to total up the $72,300 sales and another 10 minutes to prepare the papers. Then, to my surprise, he reached into his briefcase again and pulled out a checkbook. He wrote a check in full and said, "Please have the cars ready to pick up at five p.m. tomorrow. I'll bring my family in to drive them home, and I'll sign the rest of the papers then. That should give you time for my check to clear." With that, he stood up, shook my hand and departed.

The gross profit on the deal was $10,350, and I received 35%, a $3,600 commission. That was close to my total monthly commissions at the time.

Just a personal note here. If he had read this book and used the principles I've outlined, he could have saved several thousand dollars.

There are many stories to be told of unusual experiences in the car business. But they are nearly all based on the interaction between customer and salesperson. If BOTH are properly trained and educated about the auto industry, a fair and acceptable purchase can be made and the professional salesperson can make an honest living.

In *Time* magazine (July 25, 1994), Paul Gray wrote an

excellent article about the new breed of sales representatives showing up at dealerships across the country. "They are experimenting with the novel idea that honesty is the best policy," said Gray.

In that same article, Ken Winkleman, an instructor for Oldsmobile, asked members of one of his classes to list some of the old tricks of their trade. They eagerly volunteered with the following list:

LOWBALLING: Setting a price ridiculously below dealer's cost, knowing that the customer will not find anything cheaper elsewhere, and then "uploading" the package with piffles, when the buyer returns.

DOUBLE DIPPING — Billing again for services, such as shipping and lot charges, that are already included in the sticker price.

GROUNDING — Making it almost impossible for buyers to leave the lot, employing ruses, such as fictitious waits for sales managers to arrive to dicker, or the temporary "loss" of vital car keys.

FLIPPING/TURNING OVER — Rotating customers from one sales representative to another to confuse the buyer and break down resistance.

We've already covered some of these problems; others will be addressed as we move through the pages of this book.

Word of warning here: Some of the sales representatives you'll run into are just one fry short of a Happy Meal. Be prepared.

Some fees are negotiable and some are not. I need to find out which of these fees I really have to pay.

----------Chapter Eighteen

Preps, Docs and Stuff

There are certain fees and expenses that require some discussion. Some fees are generally NOT negotiable and are part of a total agreement.

When buying a new car, you'll see a fee on the MSRP sticker that's attached to the car window, called DESTINATION CHARGE. This is part of the total cost of a new car and is a locked-in nonnegotiable amount. This figure represents the AVERAGE cost of transporting a car from the manufacturer or port of entry to the dealership.

If you buy a Mercury Sable made in either Atlanta, Georgia, or Portland, Oregon, the Destination Charge is the same. Accept it. That's the way it is.

PREP (Preparation) CHARGES cover the cost of preparing the car for delivery from the time it comes off the truck until you take delivery. This involves taking off protective wrapping, cleaning interior and exterior, and some servicing of the engine. These charges vary, depending on the make of the car. Such charges are related ONLY TO NEW CARS. Many dealers will charge prep charges on used cars. DON'T PAY IT. YOU ARE GETTING DOUBLE DIPPED. On used cars, the cost of this preparation is included in the selling price.

Prep Charges will vary in cost from $69 to $369. Currently, the average fair cost is about $149. Negotiate this charge. Some dealers will work with you and some won't. Many of them have this charge printed on their buyer's order. Watch for it.

Remember: Dealers use the same buyer's order for new and used cars and will automatically charge you the prep charge on used cars, unless you JUST SAY, "NO!"

DOC (Documentation) fees are to cover the cost of your license plate and registering your car with the state. Currently, the total cost in Georgia, for instance, is $39 plus a $3 fee for the Lemon Law Fund. This is a fund set up by the state to protect new car buyers from buying a lemon (a badly diseased car!). This fund is available in many states. Check with any local auto dealer to see if it's available in your state. Documentation fees are NOT negotiable.

If a dealer is trading a new car from another dealer, there may be some transportation costs involved. This cost should be included in the price of the car — not added on again. Remember: The cost of shipping and lot fees are already included in the selling price. Look out for more Double Dipping.

Ken Winkleman in the *Time* article, mentioned earlier, tells his students like it is: "You can shear a sheep many times in its life, but you can only skin it once." Folks who prepare themselves with education will never get sheared in the first place, let alone skinned!

Oh, by the way, here are the charges for those extras. With pin stripes and the gold package, that comes to an extra $1,000.

Chapter Nineteen

More Add-Ons

One of the things that irritate car buyers most is the deliberate buildup of the price of the car by adding on items which should be included on all cars. To best illustrate this problem, let me quote to you from Mel Bloom's article in *Los Angeles* magazine, May 1989. (Also, condensed in *Reader's Digest*.) Mel says,

> Why do some dealers have TWO stickers on the car? Those are dealer add-ons that boost the price by as much as $1,000. When a protective polish that costs $15 is applied by low-wage help, the buyer is charged $185. Pin striping runs about $7 per stripe, but you pay $75. Fabric seats are stain-protected by a $3 aerosol can, but you're charged at least $60. You're made to feel you've scored a major triumph when you can do away with the add-ons and return to the basic sticker price.

Add-ons are gimmicks designed by professionals to take advantage of amateurs. The only things on an add-on sticker should be major items, like CD systems, air conditioners, cruise control, moon roofs or other specialty items that are after-market installed and optional. These are items that are added on locally by the dealer, after the car arrives on the lot. They will not appear on the MSRP sticker. These items should be negotiated separately and bought at dealer's cost.

The latest add-on is the "Gold package." Dealers are charging as much as $800 for gold-plated emblems on new cars. They pay local companies $25 per emblem for this extra. Check your local *Yellow Pages* under "plating or trophies." They will come to you for the same price. Most cars average four emblems.

After-market products are another area where the dealers can price-gouge the customer. Again, I refer to Mel Bloom's article. A car salesman he interviewed said, "We buy fancy mag wheels for $120 and sell them for $500. Air conditioning costs the dealer $400, but you pay close to $1,000. A package of automatic windows, tilt steering wheel and cruise control costs you $1,200." Of course, this article was written in 1989. You should add at least 25% to the figures quoted.

We have been playing these price games since the Nash Rambler, and if you think they're going to change soon, I have four tickets to the 1990 Super Bowl, and I'll sell them to you today for half price.

Are you pre-approved?

Chapter Twenty

Financing Rates

Now it's time to enter an area of car buying that involves more savings than all the price wars combined. There is more money made and lost in the finance office than any other area of the business. Let's start with INTEREST RATES.

As mentioned in Chapter One, shopping in advance for the best interest rate is critical. You need to know the best rate available to you BEFORE you go to the finance office.

Where do you shop? Three common sources are your credit union, your local bank and your local finance company.

CREDIT UNION: If you have access to a credit union, I recommend you talk to them first. Find out what interest rate and time period it will take to approve you. Rate and length of the loan are connected to the *age of the car you are buying*. The older the car, the higher the interest rate and the shorter the loan period. If you can get pre-approved for a dollar amount, do it. This will give you more control when you're negotiating in the finance office.

Besides generally having the lowest interest rates, credit unions can payroll-deduct your car payments and thereby protect your credit by making sure your payments are timely.

Pardon me, if I digress. But here's an important point: PAYMENT RECORDS ON A CAR LOAN ARE THE MOST IMPORTANT INFORMATION ON YOUR CREDIT REPORT. THEY ARE EVEN MORE IMPORTANT THAN MORTGAGE PAYMENTS. PROTECT YOUR FUTURE CAR LOAN POTENTIAL BY MAKING ALL YOUR CAR PAYMENTS ON OR BEFORE THE DUE DATE. YOUR CAR-PAYMENT HISTORY WILL AFFECT YOUR INTEREST RATE AND APPROVAL ON FUTURE PURCHASES.

Now, back to credit unions. There's one possible negative feature you need to consider when using a credit union for auto purchases. Credit unions offer loans for many reasons — not just cars. Their loans are basically personal loans. They are an excellent source for emergency money for unexpected problems. If you tie up that source with a car loan, you lose that emergency source. For that reason, it may be better for you to use another source for your car loan and keep the credit union available for the unexpected.

YOUR BANK: The bank that you use for checking and savings is another prime source for car loans. They know you, and you know them. If you have existing loans, past loans or mortgages with them, that's even better. Go visit "your friendly neighborhood bankers" and tell them what you want to buy.

DO THIS BEFORE YOU START SHOPPING OR AT LEAST BEFORE YOU GO TO THE FINANCE OFFICE. Again, if you can get pre-approved, do it. You need to know your options ahead of time.

FINANCE COMPANIES: If you have credit problems, credit unions and banks are not options for you. Therefore, then and only then, you should consider checking out a finance company. THIS SOURCE SHOULD ONLY BE USED FOR INTEREST-RATE INFORMATION AND NOT TO ACTUALLY BORROW MONEY.

MOST dealerships are much better sources for financing than a finance company. This is one of the many reasons why I recommend that you avoid independent car lots, especially lots that do their own financing (often called, Buy Here — Pay Here, or Tote-Your-Note Lots). A major new car dealership has many sources for financing and more clout with these sources. They will work with your credit to get a better rate (just a little better) and can often get you approved where independent car lots cannot. And these sources won't repossess your car if you're five minutes late with a payment.

You now have your financing information in your back pocket, and your dream car is waiting outside for you. You're in the finance office ready to deal. How do you handle the finance manager, what do you say and how do you best negotiate with the finance manager with the information you have?

First, you need to know how he operates, what his goal is and how he thinks. It is the finance manager's job to have you sign his contract, containing the highest interest rate possible, the most finance options included and the longest payment terms possible.

When you settle in and finish the small talk, he will present you with a stack of papers to sign. As we continue through this book, we'll cover all of these papers. For now, though, let's concentrate on the contract. This is where the interest rate, term and payments are listed. He will have it already filled in by computer and ready for your signature. IF YOU SIGN IT NOW, YOU WILL PROBABLY LOSE THOUSANDS OF DOLLARS.

The interest rate will be elevated. The term will probably be as much as 60 months . . . STOP!

Tell the finance manager that you are already approved at (whatever you have already shopped for), and unless he can better that rate, you'll get your financing from your own source. Many dealerships, along with their special sources (Ford Motor Credit, GMAC, Chrysler Credit, etc.), also use many of the same sources that you have accessed, like local banks. They can almost ALWAYS match or better your rates.

Hold your ground. It could mean as much as a 5% to 7% savings. This could mean reducing the term of the loan from 60 months to 48 months or 42 months and not increasing your payments. The savings would be tremendous. If the finance manager matches your bank's rates, you should use the dealership's financing.

Why?

Because more money is made in the finance office than any other profit center in the dealership.

An experienced finance manager is intimidated by knowledgeable customers. You must control this part of the buying experience more than any part of your negotiations.

Finance managers and educated car buyers are as compatible as hiccups and razor blades.

I checked with my local
insurance agent, and I can get
the exact same coverage as
you are offering – except his is
seventy-five percent less!

_____ Chapter Twenty-One

Special Insurance

Now we get into an area that I enter with great passion: INSURANCE.

I have been a licensed insurance agent for the states of Georgia, North Carolina, Tennessee and Kansas; for the past 10 years, I have had my own agency. I am a true believer in many types of insurance. We need to protect our families and futures with good, sensible insurance.

I strongly believe that Credit Life Insurance and Disability Insurance, connected to auto finance contracts, is not only bad but down right FRAUDULENT. First, let me explain what these products are and what they are supposed to do for you.

CREDIT LIFE INSURANCE: This is an insurance policy that is added to your purchase contract that states — if you die, the insurance company will pay off your loan and transfer the paid-up title to your beneficiary.

Sounds good. But in reality it is nothing but a LIMITED, DECREASING-TERM LIFE POLICY WITH THE PAY OFF LIMITED TO THE CAR. The beneficiary can't take cash, and the value of the benefit decreases as the loan is paid. The cost of this policy is 5 to 8 times the cost of a simple, decreasing-term life policy; and to make it even more expensive, it's added to your loan and financed for 3 to 5 years. THIS IS A REAL RIP-OFF . . . DON'T BUY IT!

First, if you had two cars financed and you died, no one will want **your** car. You died . . . The car would carry with it painful memories. Perhaps, or more than likely, the car would be sold or traded in for another car. Since you had a loan on it, the car probably has equity and your beneficiary will have cash left over.

Second, for the same amount of money as this Credit Life Insurance, you can buy $50,000 of 5-year, level-term insurance, which means that if you die any time during the 5 years (probably the term on your car loan), your beneficiary will receive $50,000. He or she can still sell the car, pay off the loan, add the equity to the $50,000, take a trip to Europe, come home and pay cash for a new Mercedes. Now, you tell me, which is a better deal?

I personally know of only one example where a man was able to benefit from Credit Life Insurance. He was 55 years old and had terminal cancer. He was classified as totally uninsurable. Since he could buy a car and the finance managers pushed Credit Life on him with no questions asked, he bought five new Cadillac Devilles at different dealers and put Credit Life on each of them.

Three months later he died. His wife received 5 titles to 5 cars, paid in full. She sold 4 of them for $30,000 each and has some extra money to live on. Smart fellow!

Talk to your local life insurance agent about inexpensive, level-term life insurance. He is a LICENSED, experienced agent who can recommend a variety of inexpensive policies to meet your needs. Most finance managers are not licensed agents and should not be allowed to sell insurance in the first place.

ACCIDENT AND HEALTH OR DISABILITY INSURANCE: The purpose of this insurance is to make your car payments if you are sick, injured or disabled. This will protect your credit and make your payments while you're unable to work.

Again, the cost is outrageous compared to standard disability policies, and the benefit you receive is limited to your car payment. The cost is added to your loan and financed over the life of the loan.

If you become disabled, you may only have a few payments left, and your benefit would be far less than your premiums. Also, if you are so ill that you can't work, you shouldn't be driving. If you are unable to work for several months, it would be better to sell the car and use the money for medical expenses. Besides, if you're out on disability and driving around, your employer might see you and fire you for faking disability. The solution is simple.

If you feel you need disability protection, call your local LICENSED insurance agent and discuss the options available for short-term and long-term disability protection. The cost is

ONE-FOURTH that of the limited policies offered by the dealership, and the benefits are in cash to be used any way you choose, not just for a car payment.

Now that you know what these insurances are and what they're for, you need to know one more important fact. WHEN YOUR PURCHASE CONTRACT IS PRESENTED TO YOU IN THE FINANCE OFFICE, 80% OF THE TIME THESE INSURANCE BENEFITS WILL BE INCLUDED.

Look for them and get them off the contract. The cost can range from $600 to over $2,000. Add that to the amount of the car loan and finance it for 60 months, and you take from $670 to $2,230 out of your pocket — needlessly.

By the way, I suggest that you take a look at your home mortgage. Most of them include some kind of Credit Life. The same information applies here. Replace it with REDUCING-TERM LIFE INSURANCE and save thousand of dollars with no loss of benefits.

How can you tell the difference between a finance manager and a coyote lying dead in the road?

With the coyote, you usually see skid marks.

I thought the car came with a 3-year warranty. Why is the finance manager trying to sell me additional coverage?

Chapter Twenty-Two

Warranties

It is the finance manager's job to sell you warranties. Remember: He is a profit center. It's his job to make as much money as the traffic will bear. The price should be negotiated. Don't EVER accept the quoted price. A two-year/24,000-mile warranty with full coverage and a $25 deductible costs the dealer about $150. But such a deal can sell for as much as $700. This is sold on new and used cars. If you NEED it and WANT it, DEMAND a lower price.

The finance manager is trained to bury the cost of the warranty in the contract. Many will tell you that the lien holder (the company that is loaning you the money) REQUIRES a warranty to approve your loan or to avoid an even higher interest rate. They use your "not so perfect credit" as an excuse for charging higher rates or demanding a warranty. If your loan is approved through a major lending institution, THERE ARE NO STRINGS ATTACHED. You can take the loan at competitive rates with no warranty OR insurance.

Remember, on NEW CARS, they ALL come with at least a standard 3-years/36,000-mile, BUMPER-TO-BUMPER WARRANTY. This is included in the price of the car and is not an extra cost to you. This warranty is all you need for the first 3 years or 36,000 miles. Any other warranty you buy will overlap that period and have no value to you.

Think hard, if you are financing, as to whether or not you want to finance a 2-year warranty for 5 years with interest. All warranties start from the date of purchase and the existing mileage, not after the factory warranty runs out.

IMPORTANT: IF THE CAR STILL HAS UNUSED MILES UNDER THE FACTORY WARRANTY, THE FACTORY WARRANTY IS TRANSFERABLE TO THE NEW OWNER FOR THE BALANCE OF THE TIME OR MILES.

You can wait until the end of the warranty period, then go to any dealer and buy another warranty at that time. You may not even keep the car that long. So, in the end, an extended warranty may not be important to you.

Used cars have NO warranties. Most need some kind of basic warranty. Two years is plenty. Most people don't keep a used car much longer. If you do keep your car longer, buy another warranty. When you buy a used car, you're usually buying someone else's problems. So, cover yourself as best you can.

DON'T FINANCE A WARRANTY — PAY CASH. Why finance a 2-year warranty for 3 years or 4 years with interest, when it's only good for 2 years?

Meantime, if you are pushed or confused about anything in the finance office, BACK OFF! These people are trained professionals, and it's their job to load you down with as much extra baggage as possible. This is where they make their money — and it's all at YOUR expense.

Let me give you an example of a dealer who got rich using his professionalism in the finance office. The finance manager devised a great plan to offer to everyone who purchased a car in his dealership. Since everyone who bought a new or used car had to be processed through his office, the finance manager offered each buyer a special package. Often it was included right in the contract, and, if not questioned, wasn't discovered until weeks later.

The benefit package included a car phone, a security system, an oil change and annual auto detailing for three years for only $395. This was added to the total price, taxed and financed for the period of the loan. Sounds good, right?

Free car phones are available anywhere and most include installation. Cost to the dealer — 0. To get the security system, you paid $75 to have it installed. Cost to the dealer — 0. The oil change, after 3,000 miles, cost the dealer $6.

Most of the people who purchased a car with this "great benefit" didn't even remember they had an oil change coming. If they missed the required 3,000 miles, the offer was no good. Cost to the dealer — almost 0. As for the annual auto detailing, well, it was usually forgotten. Less than 10% of the people who took advantage of the "great benefit" (a $10 cost to the dealer) failed to take advantage of their so-called windfall. Cost to the dealer — almost 0.

The dealership netted about $375 on each sale and was able to include the package in 75% of all cars sold. They averaged about 250 car sales per month. Allow me to do the arithmetic for you. That's a clear profit of $70,300 per month less a $6,000 bonus to the finance manager. And you wonder how car dealerships can afford to stay in business!

There are many other profitable things available for the finance manager to offer you — while you're excited and in the signing mode. We'll cover those in the next chapter.

What do the letters F O R D stand for? FOUND ON ROAD, DEAD! or FIX OR REPAIR DAILY!

That security system you sold me is worthless. My son put a quarter in it, and I cranked up the car without any problem!

Chapter Twenty-Three

Other Finance Stuff

As you are starting to learn, the finance office is an interesting place. We've learned about interest rates, credit life insurance, disability insurance, warranties and rip-offs. But there's still another black pit in which your money can disappear — SECURITY SYSTEMS.

There are basically four types of systems that you need to understand; they are:

1. The standard unit that comes from the factory,

2. The type that shuts down your electrical system,

3. The alarm system, and

4. The type that sends a signal to an outside transmitter.

The first type is a unit that is installed in most new cars. It sets off a siren if a window is broken or a door is forced open. These alarms are standard equipment, and there should be no added cost to you.

The second type is commonly called an "ignition disabler." This is a system that creates a break in the electrical system, and the car can only be started by closing the gap with a special key. The key, which looks like a small plastic card, is inserted into a slot in the dashboard, completing the circuit. One of the more popular units is called PROLOCK. Many dealers buy these units and install them in all of their new cars. This is a deterrent for thieves and, most importantly for the dealer, it lowers the insurance rate on his inventory. This system has flaws, however.

Often it can be circumvented with a quarter slipped into the slot. Professional car thieves, who know this system well, can rewire the ignition in seconds, bypassing the system.

From a car buyer's standpoint, the system is already installed and the dealer is benefiting from the insurance reduction. The buyer is offered this unit in the finance office for $200 to $400. If the buyer chooses not to buy it, the dealer has the unit plugged so it can't be used. It's already paid for by the dealer. Why not just leave it alone and let the buyer benefit from it at no cost? Do you really want to pay $200 to $400 for a system so easily outsmarted?

Another ignition disabler similar to the PROLOCK is THE IMMOBILISER. This system is much more complex but still very easy to use. It is installed by trained professionals and connects to your electrical system in four random locations. There are 120 combinations for random locations, making it almost impossible for a professional thief to rewire the car in any reasonable length of time. To date, over a million of these systems have been sold and installed in cars and trucks, and not one has been stolen by breaching the system. I recommend THE IMMOBILISER and have used them in my cars. Call 1-713-897-9991 in Houston, Texas, for information on sales locations in your area. The cost is under $200, and installation is under $100.

The third type of system is the standard ALARM system. This type of unit can be bought in most auto stores and, when installed, sounds an alarm if the car is shaken or forced open. Professionals can open the hood and cut the wire to the siren in seconds.

Last, but not least, is a system called LOJACK. This system is sold in many fiance offices and is a very high-profit item. This product, when installed, emits a signal that can be picked up by police. The problem with this idea is that the police won't look for your car until you report it stolen. It only takes a thief about an hour to steal and strip your car. What do you think they take out first? The LOJACK. Meanwhile, there's a great black market for stolen LOJACKs.

If you would feel more comfortable with the LOJACK, don't buy it at your car dealership at the asking price. Shop around and pay cash. If you add it to the car deal, you'll be financing it for four or five years.

The finance office is a dangerous place for the unprepared buyer. Review the information in this book again before leaving home to shop for your next car. You'll be dealing with the pros. But you can CONTROL your wallet or purse, now that you know what to expect.

You know what you have when you find a hundred finance managers at the bottom of a lake? A good start!

The ad says I can lease my favorite car for $199 per month, but to buy the same car will cost me $289 per month. What to do?

_____Chapter Twenty-Four

Leasing vs. Buying

One of the most common question I'm asked is this: "Should I lease or buy?"

Before I can answer this mind-boggling question, we need to understand exactly what leasing is.

Here are the major differences between owning a vehicle and leasing a vehicle.

When you purchase a vehicle, you make a down payment and finance the balance from a lending institution at a fixed rate of interest for a fixed period of time. At the end of that period, the lending institution releases your title to you, which was held in escrow, and the vehicle is yours alone.

When you lease a vehicle, you put down only the first and last month's payments and usually a security deposit. The leasing company owns the vehicle and retains the title in their name for a fixed period of time — usually 2, 3, 4 or 5 years. The dealership from which you lease will estimate the value of the vehicle at the end of the fixed period. That amount is called the RESIDUAL. When that fixed period is over, you have four options:

1. You can turn the car in and end the lease;

2. You can purchase the vehicle for the residual amount;

3. You can purchase the vehicle by financing the residual amount for a fixed period of time at an agreed interest rate; or

4. If the vehicle is worth more than the residual value, you can use it as a down payment on a new purchase or a new lease.

There are two kinds of leases: (1) open end; and (2) closed end.

On an open-end lease, the residual can be adjusted up or down at the end of the lease, depending on the market at the time. My advice is to STAY AWAY FROM OPEN-END LEASES. They can cost you nothing but money and grief.

The closed-end lease has a fixed residual, and you can walk away clean, no matter what the value is at the end of the lease. If the value drops below the residual, you are protected from loss. If the value is higher than the lease, you have equity and can either pocket it or use it as down payment on a new or used vehicle. INSIST ON A CLOSED-END LEASE.

Warranties, credit life and disability insurance are optional on leases. If the leasing company thinks you should have these options, JUST SAY, "NO!" If they want it to protect their lease, let them buy their own. These options will automatically be included in the first agreement. So, be sure to have them removed.

Many leases have a hidden fee called a TERMINATION FEE; it costs about $250. Leasing companies charge consumers this termination fee if they decide not to buy the car at the end of the lease.

"This fee should really be called a disposition fee, because it's the cost the company incurs to dispose of the car, like sell it or take it to auction," says Dick Biggs, past president of the National Vehicle Leasing Association. "This should always be in the lease agreement, but since most people don't read every line of the agreement, they don't realize they'll have to pay it. In addition, some leasing companies also charge you a fee to get out of a lease early."

Beware of double-dipping here. Read the agreement carefully. Take it home and make notes if you're not sure what you're signing. Have the finance manager explain every detail. Leases vary like people.

ALL LEASES INCLUDE GAP INSURANCE at no additional cost to the lessee. Gap insurance is included to protect you from loss if you are in an accident and the car is totaled. The insurance companies will not give you enough to replace your car. Gap insurance will make up the difference. Some dealers will try to double-dip you by charging you for this gap insurance as an add-on to the lease. Don't get caught.

It is important to know that a lease agreement DOES NOT show the price you're paying for the vehicle OR the interest rate you're paying. The only thing listed will be the amount of payments and the length of the lease. You must insist on seeing a form, which is a WORKSHEET. You must be able to see how the dealer developed the payments.

The worksheet should break down the price you have negotiated on the car you're leasing, the interest rate you have agreed upon, the residual amount agreed upon and the payment period you've agreed upon.

Now let's talk about how to negotiate your lease. To determine the price of the car, you should negotiate it as if you were BUYING it. As a matter of fact, I would tell the salesperson that you want to buy the car from the beginning. You need to negotiate the LOWEST price possible. We'll get into the art of negotiating in the next chapter. For now, though, you need to negotiate your trade separately and get the MAXIMUM price for it. Decide on whether or not you want to put any cash into the deal and how much. You will, of course, already know your best available interest rate.

Now you have all the pieces of the puzzle and can start putting them to work for you. Subtract your trade value and any cash down from the agreed purchase price of the new car. Then subtract the residual value. Add the security deposit, the first and last payment, and the prep charge. The bottom line should represent the amount that you will be financing:

Let's create an example.

AGREED PURCHASE PRICE ON NEW CAR	$20,000.00
AGREED TRADE-IN VALUE ON YOUR OLD CAR	5,000.00
CASH DOWN	1,000.00 -
SECURITY DEPOSIT	300.00 +
FIRST & LAST PAYMENT	500.00 +
PREPARATION CHARGE	200.00 +
AGREED RESIDUAL	7,500.00 -
AMOUNT TO BE FINANCED ON LEASE	$7,500.00

Now we can get out our payment book and calculate the payment based on $7,500.00, multiplied by the agreed interest rate, for the number of months you have chosen to lease.

If you don't review these calculations, you will be presented a blind lease that will generally be based on the MSRP sticker, minimum wholesale on your trade, a high interest rate and a higher residual. This could affect your payments by as much as $100 per month. I have personally adjusted lease payments in excess of $100 per month, and this deception is almost standard practice. This is another reason you NEVER buy based on payments.

As to whether you should lease or buy, I am not an advocate of leasing. Here's why . . .

50% OF ALL PEOPLE WHO CALL ME WITH PROBLEMS ARE PEOPLE WHO ARE TRAPPED IN LEASES. THERE IS NO ESCAPE!

In these modern times, our lives are changing almost daily. We get promoted, demoted, moved, increase and decrease our family size, get rich or go broke. Once you are locked into a lease, there is no way out without losing a lot of money. If you must lease, keep the lease period as short as possible. I recommend no more than two or three years.

You need to know another fact about financing a lease. You need excellent credit to get a lease approved. The requirements are much higher than those for a purchase. If your credit is shaky, you'll probably have no choice but to buy rather than lease.

Most advertising on radio, television and newspapers is based on lease pricing; Why? Because it looks cheaper and easier. But read that fine print. Beware of the good old BAIT AND SWITCH.

If the offer looks too good to be true, it probably is!

The Chevy Nova never sold well in Spanish-speaking countries. "No va" means "It doesn't go" in Spanish.

Just sign on the dotted line . . .

_____Chapter Twenty-Five

Negotiating

There's an art to negotiating. Here's a question that illustrates the importance of knowing what to say and when to say it.

You have done your homework, chosen your car and you're ready to deal. The salesperson offers to sell you the car at full manufacturer's suggested retail price and you, of course, say, "No!" His response will usually be, "What do you think would be a fair price for your car?"

The MSRP is $18,000, and you would like to buy it for $15,000, based on your research. How do you answer this boggling question without it costing you big bucks?

If you say any amount more than $12,000, YOU LOSE! No matter how ridiculous it may sound, that is where YOU must start YOUR negotiations. Your price is just as crazy as his price. Your price is exactly the same distance from your target as his price is. The salesperson started $3,000 over your goal, and you must start $3,000 under your goal.

Now the fun begins, and you are in control. Every time he comes down on the price, you can come up an equal amount without compromising your target price. After long consultations with his manager, he will probably drop to $17,000. You can then reluctantly agree to buy at $13,000. After another meeting, he comes back with his final and best offer of $16,500. You counter with your final and best offer of $13,500. At this point, you want to remind the salesperson that you're only $3,000 apart. Surely they can be competitive with their friends across town and at least come close to their price of $14,800. The sales manager now gets into the act personally and says, "The best I can do is $15,500. Take it or leave it!"

Here you say, "But we're only $700 apart. I hate to have to drive across town to buy, but you can understand that to save a few hundred dollars, it's worth it to me. I appreciate your efforts and understand that you can't always be competitive." Then, GET UP AND LEAVE.

Fifty percent of the time you won't get past the door. Twenty-five percent of the time, you won't get out of the drive. Ninety percent of the time, your answering machine will have a message on it, asking you to come back in, since the dealership found a mistake in their figures. You are still in control.

Go back on your terms and split the difference. Even if you are $300 to $500 above your target price, you have won, since your target should have been a little low anyway.

Sometimes you can't move the dealership all the way to

your price because of availability or popularity of the car you expect to purchase. The important thing to remember here is that by using the methods demonstrated above, you have control of the results. Had you offered to buy at your target price, you would have lost on the first compromise. Leaving without burning bridges will leave the door open to swing both ways. If the dealership doesn't call you back in, you know they can't come down any more, and you probably have the best deal available at the time.

Whether you're negotiating the price of a new or used car, the warranty or financing, use the same methods. If your interest rate goal is 9%, and you are offered 10.5%, you counter with 7.5%. You know that he can match your bank's 9%. For instance, I'd even suggest that your bank is offering a little lower rate than they are to entice a more competitive rate. Settle at YOUR target — not theirs.

The key to successful negotiating is CONTROL. Whoever gets and maintains control will win the battle for YOUR buck.

From the time you step on a dealer's lot, the salesperson is taught to establish control of your every thought and action. A real PRO can sell you a pink VW at $5,000 over sticker with 30% financing and have you walk away five hours later with a smile on your face, anxious to tell your friends what a great deal you got. Believe me, both P. T. Barnum and that salesperson know your name.

Some of the key areas to control which a good salesperson is taught in "Basic Car Sales 101" are:

1. "Sell what is on the lot."

It is the salesperson's job to move inventory that is on the dealer's lot. Remember, your strategy is that you have a dealer-trade benefit, and you can insist on buying exactly what YOU want. Cars which meet your requirements can be located in minutes from anywhere in your region. This usually represents a 300-mile radius of your city.

2. "Don't let them off your lot until they either buy or they are TO'd (turned over) to a manager. Customers are like robots; they'll do whatever you tell them."

   Your strategy as a smart car buyer is to keep your keys and know where your car is at all times.

3. "Demonstrate the car on YOUR route."

   We've discussed this. Break their pattern. As the carbuyer, you have the right to try it out on the expressway or wherever YOU'RE comfortable.

4. "Sit them down in your cubical and work them."

   Knowledgeable buyers don't get pinned in. Always be in a position to get up and leave at your will.

5. "Control the keys."

   You know this one.

6. "Don't let the customer procrastinate. Close it now."

   Take your time, be sure you are doing the right thing. It's your money being spent here. Remember what the

famous southern belle said in *GONE WITH THE WIND,*
"Tomorrow is another day."

7. "Don't discuss price. Always sell on payments."

    You don't want to discuss payments, only price. Don't
give him a budget to manipulate.

I realize that there is an overwhelming amount of
information here, and you can't absorb and use it all on your
first car quest. By being aware of how the competition works
and thinks, though, you can get and retain control of your car
deal and, in turn, your money.

A mother and her son were walking through a cemetery
and passed by a headstone inscribed "Here lies a good
car dealer and an honest man." The little boy looked
up at his mother and asked, "Mommy, why did they
bury two men in there?"

Another war story to entertain, amuse and educate.

Chapter Twenty-Six

Break III

Time for a little break!

You've been besieged with information for several chapters. Let me pass along to you another war story. This one occurred just a few years ago during a consultation.

I was at a local television station doing a guest appearance. After the program, one of the engineers came up to me and asked for some advice. He had already bought a new car, and after reviewing the contract almost a week later, was concerned that he didn't get the deal he thought he should have.

I looked over the contract and, as expected, found that he had been hit with what is called in the industry, THE FULL BOAT. He had included in the contract: credit life, disability insurance, a warranty, an inflated interest rate, 60-month payment period and only about $500 off the MSRP price. Besides all of this, there was a $500 rebate at the time, which was never mentioned.

Since he was an employee of a popular television station, I talked with the program manager and asked if I could have a camera crew and reporter, if needed, to clean up this matter and present an interesting consumer-news piece. The program manager was agreeable to my proposition. Therefore, I set up an appointment with the sales manager to meet with my client, the engineer and me — to review the contract for clarification.

That evening, the engineer from the TV station and I sat down with the sales manager. I introduced myself, saying, "As you probably know, Mr. Jones is an engineer at WCAR-TV." (The names and the station have been changed to protect all concerned.) "I am a consumer reporter for the station." (I am a reporter, but not for any television station, though in the moment I was.)

"We would like to redo this contract. I'm sure you are aware of the discrepancies on it."

As expected, the sales manager thought everything was in order and didn't understand how anyone would NOT be happy with the great deal my client had. I began listing the items that needed to be changed, and after he tried to argue his case, I looked him straight in the eye and said with conviction, "If we can't agree on these errors, I have a camera crew standing by, and we can get an Emmy for the show this encounter can create."

His tone changed dramatically. The old contract was quickly replaced with a new, streamlined contract.

When we finished up, the contract went from $385 per

month to $270 per month. The payment period went from 60 months to 54 months. That created a savings of $8,520 for my client, the TV engineer. To say that he was happy is putting it mildly.

The reason I tell this true story is to reemphasize to you the importance of learning all you can about car buying. Auto dealers are robbing the untrained public blind. Pass this book around to your friends who may be in the market for a car. Let them know that you care. Of course, I'll be happier if they go out and buy their own copy. But get this information into their hands as soon as you can.

I am on a crusade (call me Don Quixote, if you like), but you can join my crusade by spreading the word. We're not talking grocery coupons here. We're talking SERIOUS MONEY!

HONDA: Had One — Never Did Again.

BUICK: Big Ugly Indestructible Car Killer.

What about the new, no-haggle used car sales lots?

_____ Chapter Twenty-Seven

The Marketplace

Here is where I discuss the auto market and try to give you some of my input on the new and, supposedly, improved concepts in marketing being introduced today.

As you know, there are basically three types of locations that offer new or used cars for sale: Used Car Lot; Auto Dealership; and The Individual. We have already discussed the pros and cons of these sources.

In an effort to dominate the used car market, large corporations and conglomerates are now entering the marketplace with big bucks, offering huge inventories, elaborate showrooms and special warranties on used cars. Big names in this new approach include CARMAX (owned by Circuit City), KARS YES (a franchise), and DRIVER'S MART (a consolidation of auto dealerships).

CARMAX was the first on the scene with five key locations in Richmond, Virginia, Raleigh and Charlotte, North Carolina, and Kennesaw and Norcross, Georgia. Because of their success during their test-market period, they are now expanding into Orlando, Tampa, Baltimore, Houston, Dallas-Fort Worth and Miami.

They offer large inventories (500 or more used cars), affordable financing, NO-HAGGLE PRICING, NO-HAGGLE TRADE-IN, 30-DAY, NO-HAGGLE WARRANTIES, five-day money back guarantee, 110-point inspection, access to auto insurance and a "Kids Only" play area.

Some of these innovations are very good. But you are paying dearly for convenience. By not being able to negotiate your car and trade, you could be overpaying by hundreds, even thousands of dollars for your total deal. You can still do better on your own at a dealership that allows you to haggle price. I would still recommend having any used car inspected by an INDEPENDENT mechanic. While this new concept is still in its infancy, I would be careful about accepting it as the wave of the future. You still get what you pay for, and it's still a buyer-beware industry.

KARS YES is a new franchise jumping on the bandwagon to compete with CARMAX. Their basic concept is the same — to offer a large inventory and variety for one-stop shopping. The same warnings apply to them. Beware of the NO HAGGLE deals.

A group of the nation's biggest car dealers is planning to open 100 huge used car dealerships. The chain currently slated to be called DRIVER'S MART WORLDWIDE, INC. will stock 350 to 650 late-model used cars and trucks. The plan is to offer

DETAILED warranties and FIXED PRICES with NO BARGAINING PERMITTED, according to Thomas Eggleston, the chain's chief executive. Driver's Mart will be jointly owned by nine car dealers who currently own a total of 118 dealerships with a combined revenue of more than $3 billion.

Some auto-industry analysts have begun to worry that — as used cars become close substitutes for new cars — automakers will find it harder and harder to raise prices for their new vehicles without losing customers. To that I say, "Hallelujah!" I have always recommended that the best buy today is not a NEW car, but a year-old USED car. If this new approach will hold down prices, the public needs the break.

However, my personal opinion regarding this new concept, is this: I can't imagine that a used car company, run by the nine largest car dealers in the U.S., is going to be run much differently than today's questionable industry standards.

A shark is still a shark, even if it's dressed as a goldfish.

_ _ _ _ _ _ _ Chapter Twenty-Eight

Sales Training

If you're going to compete with the professional car salesperson for the best buy on a car or truck, you need to know your competition.

The car salesman is a unique breed. He works long hours, weekends, rain or shine, summer or winter. He is in competition with an abundance of other salespersons with you as the prey. Generally speaking, all salespeople are starving, inadequately trained, degraded, tired and disenchanted. Nearly 80% have changed employers in the past nine months. Over 30% have never sold cars before, and about 80% wish they could get rich some other way.

Don't despair! There are still about 20% who know the difference between a Ford and a Chris Craft. Now this may sound satirical, but the truth needs to be told.

I have been involved with the sales and management of vehicles for over 20 years, and the "80% Factor," as I call it, is a serious problem in the industry. Eighty percent of America' auto sales force is comprised, in large part, of inexperienced men and women who have never worked closely with the public, have never been properly trained or can't find any other source of income. They are chasing the "silver lining" or "the carrot," created by false promises of auto sales management.

I have worked with alcoholics, drug addicts, ex-cons, runaway dads and even an admitted drug pusher. Don't panic. Working in the same industry, I have also met and worked with some of the finest, most honest, caring and sincere people I have ever known. Over the years I have sorted out many of the true professionals who make up about 20% of the sales force.

Over half of the nonprofessionals have worked for at least two different car dealers in the past year. Many have a long list of different dealers on their résumé. This nomadic problem is not all the fault of the salespersons, however. The dealers add fuel to the problem in many ways:

1. They don't train their recruits adequately;

2. They don't properly screen applicants;

3. They readily accept high turnover;

4. They degrade new salespersons and control incomes;

5. They play carrot games with bonuses and incentives; and

6. They overhire, therefore limiting opportunity for survival.

Too many dealers follow the concept, "If 20 salespeople can sell 100 cars per month, then 40 salespeople can sell 200 cars." This theory almost always starves out 15 salespeople. I know of a major dealership with stores all over the country whose policy is to fire the least two productive salespeople at the end of each month, regardless of past successes.

My advice to you as a car buyer is to interview your salesperson, get to know a little about him or her. Ask questions. If he or she doesn't know the product or can't do business in a professional manner, seek out another salesperson. You are entitled to work with a professional. You're the customer.

Seek out that 20 percent. Ask who the top salesman was the month before. Most dealerships have plaques listing monthly winners. Many have progress charts on display. Ask the sales manager or the owner to recommend their best salesperson. Better yet, ask them which person has been at that dealership the longest.

Don't get caught up in the dealer's "up" system. Every day a list of "on duty" salespersons is posted. As the customers arrive, the next person on the "up list" is assigned to that salesperson. Your salesperson could have just been hired from some used car lot down the road. He may not even know where the restrooms are yet.

The biggest problem the dealerships create is that whenever they accidentally hire those "real" sales professionals, they usually promote them quickly to management, where their sales talents are wasted. Not all sales professionals make good managers and not all managers are good sales professionals.

I have seen the results of misplaced sales professionals in my work in legal cases around the country. I am occasionally hired as a professional witness in cases against dealerships which are being sued by customers for various reasons. Inexperienced sales managers are often put in a position where they must make decisions for which they're not properly trained. This puts them at odds with the car buyer, and their bad decisions are cause for legal recourse.

Take your time. Don't feel that you must walk in and buy the first car that looks good to you. Seek out a professional to answer your questions, someone who can help you zero in on what YOU need and want. With the training you now have, you can work WITH that person and put together the best deal for you, THE CUSTOMER!

The biggest problem with bucket seats is that not all people have the same sized bucket. (Thanks, Mom.)

If you find a car with a three-digit V.I.N., buy it quick. It probably belonged to Abe Lincoln himself.

_____Chapter Twenty-Nine

V. I. N. Numbers

V.I.N. stands for VEHICLE IDENTIFICATION NUMBER. This number is similar to your Social Security Number, in that it gives your car its sole identity. No other car has the same number. The V.I.N. is located in six places on a vehicle. The most common are on the dashboard in front of the steering wheel and on the driver's door near the locking mechanism. Other locations include the top of the gas tank, on the firewall, on the engine block, out of sight, and on the frame.

Many cars which are stolen are stripped and sold for parts. These parts are then often sold to body shops and put into other cars. The V.I.N. is like a fingerprint and can be traced to its original owner. Ask any car thief. The V.I.N. is often a thief's downfall.

Besides giving your car an identity, the V.I.N. can also give you some important history. For those of you buying used cars, it will tell you when the car was manufactured. This is important to know, since the price is directly related to the age of the car. For new and used car buyers, you will need this number to notify your insurance company of your purchase and to have your newly purchased car insured. All insurance policies must have your V.I.N. on them.

When reviewing your paperwork in the finance office, check the V.I.N. carefully to make sure it is correct. A mistake could cause problems later. THERE ARE 17 NUMBERS AND LETTERS IN A V.I.N. Here is an example of what one would look like and what each number or letter represents.

(Note, the next two lines should be in big letters and positioned as I have positioned them.)

A. Manufacturer and Make
    "JT stands for Japan Toyota" and is invariable.
    Example: First number or letter is nation of origin.
        Second letter is manufacturer.

B. Type of Vehicle
    Designation 2 — Passenger Vehicle
    3 — Multipurpose Passenger Vehicle
    4 — Truck
    5 — Incomplete Vehicle

C. Engine
   Example: M — 5M-GE
   S — 2S-E or 3S-GE

D. Line
   Example: T — Celica
   E — Corolla

E. Toyota Model Code
   Example: (ST)6 — ST162 model
   (SV)1 —SV11 model

F. Series (Grade
   Example: 1 — STD
   2 — DLX, LG
   3 — ST
   4 — GT

G. Body Type / Restrain System
   Example: D — 2-door Sedan
   E — 4-door Sedan
   C — Coupe
   L — Lift Back

H. Check Digit
   A single number or a letter X(10) computed by the formula
   specified in the requisition.

I. Model Year
   Example G — 1986
   H — 1987
   J — 1988
   K — 1989

L — 1990
R — 1994
S — 1995

J. Plant of Manufacturer

K. Frame Number

For the used car buyer, count from the right to the left EIGHT digits. That is the most important digit. It represents the year the vehicle was manufactured. That does not necessarily mean the model year.

On the driver's door jam is another piece of identification called the warranty identification card. This plaque has additional information that includes the paint code (so you can match your paint correctly), trim style, air conditioning code, radio code and ordering district. It also contains your V.I.N. It's usually more convenient to read than the one near your windshield.

If you find an older car with a three digit V.I.N. on it, BUY IT QUICK! It was probably made the year I was born and driven by Abe Lincoln himself. I think he called them Ford, after one of his favorite theaters. But don't quote me on that!

Hey, there, car salesmen. I've got the keys, the knowledge and the CONTROL. You'll never rip me off again!

----------------Chapter Thirty

Control, Control

Now it's time to summarize this basket of information and review the material in an orderly fashion. We have covered a lot of money-saving ideas, and you need to put them in order. The next chapter will give you 25 tips that you can use as a quick reference. Chapter names will refer to specific areas of savings. If you are shopping new cars, some chapters are not important. If you are shopping used cars, a chapter like "REBATES, REBATES" might not be important to you.

Keep in mind the progression and order of the process:

1. Prepare in advance;

2. Shop at your convenience; buy at special times;

3. Pick a professional salesperson;

4. Choose what YOU want;

5. Negotiate car and trade separately;

6. In finance — work rate, terms, warranties, extras, price, to YOUR advantage; and

7. Drive away a happy camper.

Now that you are a seasoned car buyer, go in there with a positive attitude and loads of self-confidence. You know that if you get cornered, you can get up, leave and regroup. You now know more than 80% of the sales "professionals" with whom you might deal. Now it's time to LET THE SELLER BEWARE!

If you should need more information for your specific adventure, you are welcome to write to me at C. C. I., Box 770, Roswell, Georgia 30075. I will be happy to hear from you and will respond as quickly as possible. As I mentioned at the beginning of this book, this is an ongoing crusade of mine, and my goal is to help as many friends as I can to overcome the pitfalls of buying a car.

Bumper Snicker:

My other car is a Schwinn

Before I go I should review everything Bob Blazak has taught me. I know that a prepared buyer is a buyer who SAVES MONEY.

Chapter Thirty-One

Final Review

As a final review, I'm going to give you a list of tips that you can use as a quick reference. They summarize the chapters in this book and will act as reminder for things that are of key importance to you in your buying efforts. I'll place a chapter reference after each tip, so you can reference the book for more information as you should need it.

1. BEFORE you shop, know WHAT you want, WHAT your budget is and WHAT the bank's interest rate is on new and used cars. Get pre-approved, if you can. (Chapter One)

2. Beware of BAIT ADS that you see on television or in newspapers. A tiny disclaimer will give a stock number. That car will either be gone when you get there or will be a base car with no options or options no one wants. MOST dealers use this type of advertising. (Chapter Two)

3. Shop on YOUR time. Negotiate and buy during the LAST TWO DAYS of the month and the LAST TWO WORKING HOURS of the dealership. (Chapter Three)

4. DON'T spend any money preparing your car for trade. Swap out new tires, radios and trailer hitches with friends for extra cash. Minimize your losses. (Chapter Four)

5. DON'T GO ALONE; TAKE SOMEONE WITH YOU. (Chapter Six)

6. DON'T GET ATTACHED to a car before you buy. (Chapter Five)

7. Buy used cars from lots connected to new car dealerships. They keep only the best trade-ins. (Chapter Seven)

8. Get new and used car prices from the library, bookstore or another dealer, or insist on seeing the dealer's invoice. Remember, the dealer can survive selling HIS new cars at HIS invoice. (Chapter Eight)

9. Ask competitive dealers about rebates and incentives BEFORE you deal. Keep these rebates OUT of the negotiations and deduct them from the bottom line. (Chapter Nine)

10. Don't buy a used car from ANYONE without having it checked out by an independent mechanic. (Chapter Eleven)

11. BUY ON PRICE — NOT PAYMENT. Dealers can disguise the real cost of a car by manipulating the down payment, monthly payment and length of the loan. (Chapter Twelve)

12. Write down all variances, promises and add-ons ON THE BUYER'S ORDER, ESPECIALLY WITH USED CARS. (Chapter Thirteen)

13. When trading, get back the keys to your trade-in, BEFORE you start your negotiations, so you can leave at YOUR will. (Chapter Fourteen)

14. The average annual mileage on a used car is 15,000 miles. MOST used cars die beyond 100,000 miles. (Chapter Fifteen)

15. If a deposit is required, give a MAXIMUM of $100. CASH, IF YOU CAN, and GET A RECEIPT. (Chapter Sixteen)

16. Do not get caught in the trading allowance trap. Negotiate purchase and trade SEPARATELY. (Chapter Twelve)

17. Preparation (PREP) fees cover the cost of getting your car ready for delivery after it comes off the truck. Destination fees (DOC) cover the cost of delivering the car from manufacturing plant to dealership. These fees are usually NOT negotiable. (Chapter Eighteen)

18. REFUSE to pay for add-on items like undercoating, fabric and paint protection, or items which should be included with all cars. (Chapter Nineteen)

19. Find the cost of tag and title from a competitor. (Chapter Twenty)

20. Insist that the dealer match or better YOUR bank finance rates. You can always use YOUR bank or credit union. (Chapter 20)

21. Dealers are not licensed insurance agents. DON'T BUY CREDIT LIFE OR DISABILITY INSURANCE. If you think you need it, talk to YOUR personal LICENSED insurance agent. (Chapter Twenty-One)

22. Beware of extra warranties. All new cars now have a 100% bumper-to-bumper warranty included. You can buy a used car warranty AFTER the original warranty runs out, if you still have the car. Most warranties have at least a 50% markup and all are negotiable. (Chapter Twenty-Two)

23. Leasing is not for everyone. Once you sign, you had better BE PREPARED TO KEEP THE CAR for the full lease period. Remember, lifestyles and incomes can change without warning, good AND bad. (Chapter Twenty-Four)

24. GAP INSURANCE will cover the money gap between a totaled car and a replacement car on leases. It is INCLUDED in most leases. Do not get DOUBLE-DIPPED. (Chapter Twenty-Three)

25. GET AND MAINTAIN CONTROL through the entire buying experience. Remember, it's YOUR hard-earned money being spent, and YOU CAN WALK AWAY ANY TIME YOU FEEL UNCOMFORTABLE. (Chapter Thirty)

I was giving a lecture to 250 high school students on car buying. I asked the group, "When's the best time to buy a car?"

From the mass of earrings and hormones came a sprout of wisdom as a voice rang out, "When you've got the money!"

There's hope for the future leaders of our country.

About the Author

Robert M. Blazak has been researching the auto industry for over 15 years. He has spent considerable time with several dealerships learning their selling techniques and business procedures. While working for Ford, General Motors, Chrysler and Mitsubishi, he won awards for selling which included "Salesman of the Year" and "Sales Professional" for the Ford Motor Corporation.

Mr. Blazak gained much of his information and experience after being formally trained and certified at a recognized Finance and Insurance Training School in Atlanta, Georgia. As business manager at a dealership in Atlanta, he observed serious improprieties in the industry.

His desire is to counsel students and readers, prior to their purchase of an automobile, in an effort to help them save as much of their hard-earned money as possibly. Literally thousands of dollars are needlessly lost every time an uninformed buyer closes a car sale.

In an effort to support his cause, Mr. Blazak formed a consulting Company in Atlanta — Carbuyer Consultants, Inc. The company offers advice on the telephone as well as a complete buying service that includes locating the new or used vehicle of the buyer's choice, negotiating that vehicle and trade, arranging the best financing possible and personally overseeing the paperwork and delivery. Formed in 1986, he and his staff have helped hundreds of car buyers overcome and avoid the nightmares and pitfalls, both emotional and financial, of buying a car.

In addition to his corporation, Mr. Blazak has given hundreds of lectures and seminars to civic and social groups on the subject of "How to Buy a Car." He also teaches a class, Carbuying 101, at colleges, universities and high schools in the Atlanta area.

Over the past few years, Mr. Blazak has helped produce consumer information segments for television news programs, has been a featured guest on radio and television talk shows and has spoken to a number of large organizations.

Mr. Blazak is on a "crusade" to help the consumer save money and avoid the hassles forced on the buying public by the auto industry.